Early Praise for *Abuse & Energy*...

"*Abuse & Energy* teaches the tools of healing the soul injured by abuse, trauma, hurtful family dynamics, and the dissociative reaction that impacts those who are abused and those who use energy abusively to hurt others. Mariane Weigley adds important and valuable understanding from her firsthand experience of less frequently discussed kinds of abuse: withholding, enabling, neglect, and isolation, in which energy is used, often quite subtly, to abuse.... If healing is to be complete, the spirit—energy encoded with information about *who we really are*—must be accessed fully. Mariane insightfully offers lay and professional readers a powerful glimpse of a complex territory right at the intersection of body, mind, and spirit." *(Excerpt from the Foreword)*

— JANICE DECOVNICK, PhD, Clinical Psychologist
Member, American Psychological Association

"As a psychologist and facilitator of growth, I have had the pleasure to be a part of this long journey of which Mariane speaks. I have watched as this person grew from a tightly closed flower to an open blossom that has many dimensions and is full of light and energy. She writes with heart, honesty, and integrity. I have witnessed her healing and her ability to become filled with peace, harmony, strength, and safety. I am proud of her and her ability to now live life to the fullest.

"*To each reader*: I hope that this book gives you the courage to start on your personal road to healing and recovery from the pain in your life be it physical, emotional, mental, or spiritual."

— JO ANN COOPER, PhD, Psychologist
Member, American Psychological Association
Diplomate, American Academy of Pain Management
Fellow, American College of Forensic Examiners

"Through the sharing of her own journey of childhood emotional abuse, Mariane sheds new light on the resulting adult fragmentation which occurs. She demonstrates methods of reuniting with your 'missing parts' to become whole again and able to achieve your life's full potential."

— SHARON SILLIVEN-REILEY, LMFT, CT

"Do you know anyone (could be yourself, a family member, or friend) who has been persecuted, controlled, manipulated, or bullied? If so, this enlightening, inspiring book will open their eyes to the insidious, far-ranging impact of that emotional abuse. More importantly, it will show how to regain the confidence and courage to create the quality of life you want, need, and deserve . . . now, not someday."

— SAM HORN, Author, *Tongue Fu!*® and *Never Be Bullied Again*

ABUSE
& ENERGY

Bringing You Home Through the
Transformational Power of Energy

MARIANE E. WEIGLEY, JD

You are more than you *think* you are.

Abuse & Energy™ *Series*

Weigley PUBLICATIONS, INC.
SAN FRANCISCO, CALIFORNIA

© 2016 Mariane Weigley, JD

All rights reserved. Except for the quotation of brief passages for review, no portion of this book may be reproduced, stored in a retrieval system, or transmitted in any form or by any means, electronic, mechanical, photocopy, recording, scanning, or other without the prior written permission of the publisher.

Weigley Publications, Inc.
2398 Pacific Avenue, Suite 207
San Francisco, California 94115

www.WeigleyPublications.com
www.MarianeWeigley.com

Cover design: Shannon Bodie, BookwiseDesign.com
Cover photography: Jacob Hand Photography, JacobHand.com

ISBN 978-0-9884990-0-3

Printed in the United States of America

Publisher's Cataloging-In-Publication Data
(Prepared by The Donohue Group, Inc.)

Names: Weigley, Mariane E.
Title: Abuse & energy : bringing you home through the transformational power of energy / Mariane E. Weigley, JD.
Other Titles: Abuse and energy
Description: San Francisco, California : Weigley Publications, Inc., [2016] | Abuse & energy series | Includes bibliographical references.
Identifiers: ISBN 978-0-9884990-0-3
Subjects: LCSH: Energy psychology. | Vital force. | Psychological abuse. | Self-actualization (Psychology) | Intuition.
Classification: LCC RC489.E53 W45 2016 | DDC 616.89--dc23

To My Children

Acknowledgments

On January 2, 1999, I began to write what would eventually evolve into this book. It took many twists and turns, but I never gave up. Along the way, I met many people who believed in my writing and helped me with this endeavor. This story might not have been told but for their continued emotional support. Of these many people, I want to especially thank Margery Sinclair, Rebecca Richardson, Elizabeth Yost, Janet R. Holman, Paulette Bakalars, Karen Schmidt, Vida Movahedi, Marilyn Lindberg, Marilyn Carroll, Jo Ann Cooper, PhD, Cherie Ewing, PhD, and Sharon Silliven-Reiley, LMFT, CT. Also, thanks to members of the book club in Milwaukee with whom I shared my earliest manuscripts and received valuable information and support in return.

A special thank you to Sam Horn who taught a fantastic class at the 2007 Maui Writers Retreat where I met incredible people who also nurtured me along the way.

A heartfelt thank you to all the people mentioned in the book either by name or by their role who helped me through it all. They were much needed.

And I want to thank my writing and publishing team: my editor Barbara McNichol, my cover and interior designer Shannon Bodie, my publishing consultant Sharon Castlen, and members of my writers' group Janice DeCovnick, PhD, and Jamie McMillin. Each of them provided more than their knowledge about writing and publishing; they gave me the necessary boost I needed to bring this project to fruition.

I will always be grateful to all of you.

Contents

Foreword 1

A Note From the Author 7

1	Introduction to Energy, How Abuse Harms	11
2	My Reaction to Trauma	19
3	The Rules of Energy Flow	45
4	Blockages Start Early On	57
5	My Mother's Death	83
6	Closing Her Estate	107
7	Restoring the Flow	131
8	The 60/40 Split	137
9	The Four Abuses Explained	149
10	The Unseen World	161
11	Relationships That Had to Change	173
12	The Process of Energetic Change	183
13	My View of All of "This"	193
14	Empowering Ways That End Reactions	199

Conclusion
Peace Begins on the Inside and Nowhere Else 205

About the Author 211

Stories

A NUMBER OF PIVOTAL STORIES IN *ABUSE & ENERGY* will become teaching references for building a new perspective. Look for these stories as you read:

A Mother's Day Peacock Feather	7
Missing Energy Pieces	27
My Chocolate Allergy	34
My Chocolate Release	36
The Crystal Coffin	37
A Wall of Spices	41
The 9/11 Tragedy	46
USS Greeneville	49
The Iceberg	138
The Second Apartment	140
"What Is My Community?"	141
Two Picnic Table Conversations	143
Dad's Funeral in 1965	146
"Mariane, Give Johnny the Toy"	147
Emotional Numbness	150
Discovering WENID	151
A Niacin Release	155

Another Iceberg Rises	157
Suicide Thoughts at Age Fifteen	162
NSF Program Certificate on My Old Bedroom Wall	163
Legs of Cement	166
"Involuntary" Wandering Eyes in the Counselor's Office	169
An "Involuntary" Part Speaks Directly to John	170
The "Ow" Game	174
The Last Straw	175
My "Shoehorn" Relationship	178
Connecting With Me	179
The Pencil	205
Two Places at Once	207
Golden Globe Vision	208

Foreword

By Janice DeCovnick, PhD

Souls live in the energy zone; it's our most fundamental level, the place where we live eternally. Energy is what we are made of.

—Mariane Weigley, JD

MAUI, 2007: A CLINICAL PSYCHOLOGIST AND AN ESTATE tax attorney met at a writers' conference. I was the psychologist writing a story of healing in poetry and photography. Mariane Weigley was the lawyer writing a whale of a story about abuse, dissociation, and transformation. Our writings had something profound in common: Energy! I sensed in Mariane a kindred spirit. Spirit is information about who we really are. Spirit is energy encoded with that information. Spirit cannot be denied without eclipsing who we really are.

Mariane's compelling story envelops the reader in a dramatic and intuitive portrayal of her life. It is a story of energy transformation, of energy eclipsed and then restored... beginning with chocolate.

Chocolate had not touched Mariane's lips until 2001, decades after an anaphylactic reaction at the age of five was pronounced a "chocolate allergy" by her doctor. Listening to her intuition forty-seven years later, Mariane suspected, instead, that an energy blockage resulting from one attack too many by her emotionally abusive mother had caused her body to go off like a bomb in childhood. Following her intuition, she tried one piece of chocolate after another until the dissociation with which she had reacted to her mother lifted. At fifty-two, she began the process of physical and emotional release and relief and restoration of who she was always meant to be.

Mariane describes a marvelous tale of transformation, of coming home, after years of dissociation occasioned by the traumas of childhood, to the person of strength and courage you will hear throughout her story. At every step along this journey, she used energetic vibration, emotion, and intuition to connect with her most deeply subconscious self, with that which is eternal.

Abuse & Energy teaches the tools of healing the soul injured by abuse, trauma, hurtful family dynamics, and the dissociative reaction that impacts those who are abused and those who use energy abusively to hurt others. Mariane adds important and valuable understanding from her firsthand experience of less frequently discussed kinds of abuse: withholding, enabling, neglect, and isolation, in which energy is used, often quite subtly, to abuse.

Mariane heart-wrenchingly tells *The Iceberg* story of a slowly surfacing, life-changing realization: *"Dissociation robs people of time, and I had lost most of my life to it."* She describes how dissociation creates odd circumstances in which things look familiar yet unfamiliar, how dissociation stifles emotional experiences of pain by creating numbness, and how dissociation can be experienced as a wish to flee, a sense of dread without content, an involuntary communication, and even an inability to move voluntarily. She teaches us how, in the energy world, dissociation looks like splits, tears, holes, and blockages in the energetic field. On a mental or psychological level, dissociation looks like a partial emotional death, emotional and mental shutdown, getting stuck. Mariane brilliantly demonstrates how the more energy blockages disrupt the flow of energy *inside* a person, the more dysfunction and disarray will be evident on the *outside* in a person's life.

Mariane's story of *Two Picnic Table Conversations* with her mother, who dropped emotional bombshells without showing any emotion and speaking nonchalantly, extraordinarily portrays how dissociation renders one voiceless, silent, in a state of disbelief about what is happening. Mariane describes how when dissociation occurs in families, people can be treated as though they were not even there and how cruelty can literally tear the soul.

Recognizing the abuse and the dissociation is a key tool in healing the soul. Mariane's stories further convey a process of energetic change that includes paying attention to where your attention has landed, accepting, and integrating what paying attention to your attention uncovers. She shows how doing so breaks down dissociation. She also describes breaking up dams of stuck energy so that a pleasurable flow of free energy allows you to be powerful and creative, and how a key part of the process of energetic change is getting your self and your choices into alignment with your soul.

The *Another Iceberg Rises* story describes how profoundly a child shuts down in the face of withholding, enabling, neglect, isolation, and abuse—to the point of dissociating the reality of who he or she is. Mariane's stories describe how the withholding of love, of comfort, of encouragement, of support in hard times searingly neglects the soul; the withholding of attention and ordinary care from a child depletes the soul. The failure to protect a child and to give a child positive energy hurts not only body and mind—it hurts the soul.

For those who have experienced a similar journey, *Abuse & Energy* provides a mirror revealing your own struggles as well as a way to use energy as you heal, transform, and overcome. Journaling, meditating, and seeing a mental health professional can spur on the energetic changes Mariane describes. But she also found that sometimes she had to fight everything her mother had taught her and her brother about women—awful, cruel, isolating, and disempowering attitudes—as well as her mother's "attitude" expressed in her legal will. Mariane drew upon her own resources—her knowledge of estate tax law, her friendships within the legal community, and her recognition of what was happening on an energy level—to fight back with a strong show of legal force. She had to combat her mother's outrageous embezzlement of her inheritance and her brother's stonewalling and bullying. In the end, she won!

Mariane writes, "*This book opens a door for a discussion of energy. . . . Abuse harms souls mercilessly, and it does it far more easily than we think.*" In my more than thirty years of treating patients who have suffered abuse in childhood and sometimes in adulthood, I have often been struck by the fact that in abuse, more than body and mind are wounded; the soul suffers profoundly as well. Mariane Weigley begins a discussion of the soul and its energetic fabric that are also tremendously harmed. Healthcare and mental healthcare professionals will find, in the pages that follow, a way of understanding trauma and what it does to the body, how it gets expressed, and how it is overcome on a deeply soulful level. Mariane's discussion goes beyond traditional Western medicine as well as beyond current concepts in the psychology of trauma: she describes the injuries to the soul and how they can be treated, transformed, and healed. Her *Missing Energy Pieces* story is a priceless description of being reunited with lost pieces of herself once energetically torn away in childhood—a rendition that is destined to become a classic in the literature on dissociation.

Mariane's nine *Rules of Energy Flow* are simple, straightforward, and universal. They ought to be listed *for all to read* on the walls of every doctor's and mental health practitioner's office, on every set of hospital discharge instructions, on every prescription pad. Neither body nor mind can function properly, nor can one feel one's own emotions when energy is so very blocked. The lack of ability to feel blocks a person's natural internal steering mechanism.

If we are to treat the whole person, medicine and the psychology/mental health field must come to recognize, understand, research, and educate our patients about our energy systems, which are as crucial to who we are as are the body and the mind. If healing is to be complete, the spirit—energy encoded with information about *who we really are*—must be accessed fully. Mariane Weigley insightfully offers lay and professional readers a powerful glimpse of a complex territory right at the intersection of body, mind, and spirit.

—*Janice DeCovnick, PhD*

Clinical Psychologist
Walnut Creek, California
Member, American Psychological Association

A Note From the Author

A MOTHER'S DAY PEACOCK FEATHER STORY

On Mother's Day in 2011, my daughter took me for a drive onto the University of California–Berkeley campus and to the Lawrence Hall of Science, a museum and research center that overlooks the campus and this California city. In front lies a massive statue of a black whale. When I saw the statue, I knew that, for the second time, I had "caught a whale." The first time happened when I came across a similar statue in Kihei, Maui, Hawaii.

I've learned that the whale represents my subconscious self and all that's within it—including everything I reveal in this book, stories I will tell, and other knowledge my "whale" wants to share.

As I stood there with my daughter, I told her about the statue's significance to me: how in 2001, after letting go of what I call my "allergy to chocolate," I felt I'd hooked a big "whale"—one that had pulled me for more than a decade. I'd never let go of that whale, although hanging on to it was sometimes difficult. Instinctively, I *didn't* let go, knowing hanging on to it was the right thing to do.

Oddly, even as I got pulled this way and that, it never felt like the "whale" itself actually wanted to get away. Seeing the two statues confirmed I had indeed "landed" it, first by leaving the mainland and going to Kihei, and then by moving to northern California to write about it.

That day, the black whale in front of the Lawrence Hall of Science seemed to be smiling. Like thousands of kids before us, we climbed on top and took photos of ourselves. What a celebratory moment!

I remember, too, how we walked around, taking in the views of the campus and city from that spectacular vantage point. Suddenly, something on the ground caught my eye. My daughter didn't see it until I picked it up—a stunningly beautiful peacock feather. How had it landed there? We didn't know. We looked around for its owner among those in the area, but no one appeared to have lost it, so I claimed the feather as mine.

At that moment, she reached into her purse to give me her Mother's Day card. On the front was a drawing of a peacock! Inside she'd written, "The peacock is rich in symbolism: Immortality symbolizing our timeless reality, Rebirth masking our inner growth and changing relationship, Guardian which our inner mother serves. Honoring the divine within you...."

I will never forget that day and its wonderfully rich symbolism for me.

I invite you to open up as you explore the chapters that follow. As you do, consider how my stories relate to you and see how you might also use energy to transform your life.

Mariane Weigly

1

Introduction to Energy, How Abuse Harms

*You won't realize you've been in something
until you start to come out of it.*

ABUSE HARMS MERCILESSLY. IT CAUSES DAMAGE—
the kind of damage that can't be repaired without understanding that it even exists. Abuse of any kind renders war on our souls. Souls live in the energy zone; it's our most fundamental level, the place where we live *eternally*.

Energy is what we're made of. Energy vibrates. So do our souls. And just as energy doesn't die, neither do our souls. Only our physical bodies die; our souls live on as energy.

When I use the word *energy,* I'm referring to the electromagnetic "light" of your inner being—the vibrational force that gives You, the spiritual You, an absolute place in the Universe. You might assume you're strictly a physical being, but You are more.

This book—my story—explores some of the many ways energy is used to abuse. In my case, it was (for the most part) the kind of abuse in which no one *physically* hurt me. Yet, coupled with silence, the abuse can deliver harmful, invisible blows that may not be recognized for decades.

> *Abuse of any kind renders war on our souls. Souls live in the energy zone; it's our most fundamental level, the place where we live eternally. Energy is what we are made of.*

Regardless of how it might first appear, my story is uplifting. I write it to explain the relationship between abuse and energy—how understanding yourself *as energy* is necessary to living a quality life, mentally and physically. Indeed, it's foundational to everything we think and do.

This book is part of a series that promotes inner peace. The three books in the series show how people can react to abuse and therefore emotionally shut down—something they should not do. My premise is that peace begins on the Inside, not the Outside. It begins *within* ourselves, when all of our intuitive abilities are intact and available for use. This includes our ability to feel our emotions, which is critical.

Specifically, by conveying my experiences since I was a child, you'll see how people have the ability to use energy to control, abuse, and disempower themselves and others. You'll also see how what once was lost can be restored. And you'll discover how to fight for yourself by trusting your intuition, your gut, your natural instinct, your higher self—whatever you call it. Eventually, you'll be able to use vibrational ways of dealing with issues that go beyond "thinking" and enter into a deeper "feeling" realm. This, I've discovered, is an infinitely effective way to resolve conflicts of all kinds. I sincerely believe you will, too.

When using your vibrational abilities, particularly emotion, you engage You at the deepest part, your subconscious level. That's where I found my buried treasure—my "light." Connecting to your subconscious links your physical life to everything You are and ever have been—the Universe, All That Is, the Other Side. *Living this way can make a big difference. It can even change EVERYTHING for you.*

My Family Difficulties

I am an attorney, a former IRS attorney, in fact. In 1988 at age forty, I went to law school to become the person I always could have been. Little did I know this was part of a transformational experience that would help me understand two subjects—abuse and energy—from an intimate perspective.

My mother was a liar and a cheat who died in 2005. In reviewing her estate, the IRS wanted to charge her with embezzlement but couldn't; she was dead. If they had charged her, then her children (my brother and I) would have had even less money to divide when her estate was resolved in 2012. That process took almost seven years—a quick timeframe compared to the time it took to resolve my father's estate. After he died in 1965, it took eleven years to complete the estate work. Indeed, because the process took so long, I was told his estate became the joke of the Walworth County courthouse. For my mother's estate resolution to take less time—well, I guess that was better.

By the end of my mother's life, my older brother, John, and I were so divided that whatever family connection we'd ever experienced was gone. Because of her stealing and desire to control, she not only destroyed his life but practically destroyed mine.

When Dad died, he'd bequeathed half of his estate to his wife with the rest to my brother and me to be split equally and put into trust until we reached age thirty. Somehow, though, our mother ended up with all of Dad's assets. Then at her death, my brother believed it all belonged to him, leaving me to sue her estate to get the inheritance I'd been owed all along.

The unfolding of lifelong difficult family events taught me firsthand how people can use energy to abuse. I experienced withholding, enabling, neglect, and isolation—to name a few of the many forms the abusive use of energy can take. While still a young child, I had built a defensive wall to protect myself. As a result, I experienced dissociation (a form of psychological numbing and disengagement) at an early age. Finally, as an adult at age fifty-two, I watched that wall crumble. Until then, I didn't know I had reacted to my mother in this defensive way. I also didn't know how many years of soulful living I had lost.

Only when the dissociation ended did I start to grow again energetically, beginning from the ages when the growing had stopped.

Looking back, I could see the way energy played out in how my mother and brother lived, in how she died, and in how I survived. If you've suffered abuse in your life, what I've learned has significant relevance for you.

Origins of My Mother's Divisive Attitude

What were the origins of the abuse I experienced growing up? My mother had an "attitude" toward me. This "attitude" was grounded in three things, one of which she was taught by my grandmother, her mother.

First, my grandmother said she'd rather have had ten boys than one girl because "boys can do something for you." That belief stuck with my mother—an only girl with three brothers—and made for suffering in her own childhood.

Second, my mother's father, my grandfather, died when my mother was only thirteen. She referred to her father as "her only friend." As a new widow, my grandmother packed up all four of her children and moved to Wisconsin, leaving behind the small Illinois town where they'd lived for years. My mother had dearly loved that town and never wanted to leave. In many ways, I don't think she ever *did* leave, even though she lived the rest of her life in Wisconsin.

Third, my mother used to refer to my brother, John, and say, "He looks like Papa." She didn't mean our own father; she meant *her* father. My mother loved both of us, but she *favored* him. She could also *control* him. It seemed in her mind that, because I was a girl, I didn't count, so she could always justify ignoring me. She'd often find reasons to push me out of her daily view and keep me at a distance.

I felt my mother's abusive attitude every day of my life, insidious in everything she did and didn't do that involved my brother and me. Although the choices she made were unfair and wrong, we lived with them. Invariably, she chose John over me. Indeed, they may even have made a deal between them years ago—that is, if he stayed with her (as he ultimately did), he'd get everything in her estate.

At the end of my mother's life, my brother and I fought over her will. Instead of a will, it should have been labeled her *attitude*. Anyone's will, I've learned as an attorney, is a written version of what that person's attitude had been for years, spoken or not. With only a slight exception, Mother's will read, "Everything to John."

Energy—At the Root of All Problems and Solutions

Today, I look at life through the lens of energy. As Pierre Teilhard de Chardin, a Jesuit priest, French geologist, and philosopher, said, "We are not human beings having a spiritual experience. We are spiritual beings having a human experience." I agree. Further, I believe we have knowledge of energy buried deep inside; it's innate to us. It can be used to abuse ourselves and others during our physical (human) experience, yet it can also heal us.

Energy can be used to abuse us during our physical (human) experience, yet it can also heal us. We have knowledge deep inside of us.

The knowledge of energy exists at a level most people don't visit frequently, if at all. With this book and the others to come, I hope to change that. Yes, energy is at the root of problems, but it's also where we'll find the solutions. We simply need to go deep enough into ourselves to find them. Understanding what abuse does *on the soul level* becomes the entryway for developing a greater understanding of yourself as energy. More than that, *abuse and how it relates to the unseen world* provides answers to many questions in society today.

Through my story—an instructive narrative—you'll learn how people can have energy blockages that restrict their own energy flow to such an extent that they have no "voice." (You may know someone who has experienced this.) Throughout, the learning takes the form of specific stories that have been listed in the front of this book. Pay special attention to these: they provide ongoing references as you explore experiences on your own or work with professionals.

Among the first is a story called My Chocolate Release story in Chapter 2. It reveals how it's possible to have what was thought to be an allergy to chocolate that was, in fact, a failure to release built-up energy. You'll see how both of these occurrences resulted from a kind of shutting down that occurred deep inside and created blockages—all in an effort to survive abusive circumstances. You'll find out how pieces of You (your soul) can "break off" and make You look energetically like a piece of Swiss cheese (having lots of holes). And you'll see how these pieces can be retrieved.

You'll learn that, when someone is healing, the real healing takes place at the energetic (soul) level. There is a process involved that is different from anything people are used to. You will read that, by trusting your intuition and by using this process I call the Process of Energetic Change (see Chapter 12), it's possible to naturally come out of whatever you might be stuck in due to a reaction to trauma you possibly don't even remember. One of the ways I reacted early on was by dissociating, and I was stuck in it for decades. The dissociation cleared up naturally by my learning to trust. Certainly, trusting your gut at a deep level like this requires patience, time, and effort—but well worth it!

Energy was at the root of my personal problems. And energy was the solution.

2

My Reaction to Trauma

I didn't know this kind of thing was possible....

By the time I was three, I had already lost pieces of myself at the energy level. Like a piece of Swiss cheese, energetically I had "holes." By the time I was five, my body stopped "releasing" the way it should. Then, when I took that one more bite of chocolate (which you'll read about), I developed what our family doctor thought was anaphylaxis, an extreme allergic reaction.

When I swelled up like a balloon, the doctor didn't realize this was my body's natural response to another of my mother's emotional attacks on me. Because I had suffered these attacks so many times, increasingly more of my own energy had become bottled up inside of me. This last incident involving chocolate triggered a major release, and I blew up like a bomb—but a bomb consisting of my own energy. It was "me" exploding.

From that point on, because my body was weakened, my natural release mechanisms (one of them being the ability to express myself) got worse. This way of being had become so extreme that I had almost no voice. Yes, I could speak, but I didn't dare speak out against my mother or even my older brother. I knew how far I could go with each of them, and that was it. I simply couldn't use my voice to save myself. Had I been able to speak up, I may have been able to break the pattern earlier than I did. But instead, it stayed with me until my mother died in March 2005. By that time, I was fifty-six years old.

What a pity. What a shame. My brother and I could have lived our lives so differently. We both had immense potential that lay on the cutting room floor of life. And I know we're not alone in this. The abuse of ourselves as energy holds us back.

My brother, John, had been a likable little boy, but as an adult, he sided with Mom in her abusive treatment of me. He thought she was right—probably because she taught him so. He had little or no idea that her behavior toward me was wrong—even that her treatment of *him* was wrong and actually damaging.

Over the years, the mental and emotional conflict within him—between who he was and who she expected him to be—took its toll and left him quite a "difficult" person to be around. He attended college for a few years but then lived with her for the remaining forty-plus years of her life. After she died, he told me he had no memories of his life before the age of eight. Perhaps that's not unusual, given what he had experienced.

The Presence of Trauma

The best word I could ever use to express what happened as my brother and I grew up is *trauma*. I didn't know then what trauma meant, but I do now. Yet, I was the lucky one. I did awaken. John never really did. Because of my mother's own upbringing, she left everyone in her path traumatized until the day each might awaken to the truth.

The desire to awaken comes in its own time.

My awakening started slowly in 1984 when I was thirty-five, and it gradually gained momentum. Finally, with a series of life-changing events, the trauma trapped in my body began to break up. That started in February 2001 when I could eat chocolate again, for reasons explained later. Yet, I hadn't tasted chocolate since I was five—and *wow*, what a powerful reaction that release caused! At that point, my body began to clean out the backlog of toxicity and then release old emotions stored inside, many of which had left me stuck.

As part of my release, my eyes teared for two weeks, the skin on the inside of my elbows became caustically sore, I itched all over, and the back of my neck was raw with irritation. That was only *part* of the physical reaction. There was more, and it took weeks to show itself.

I didn't know that maintaining a good energy flow throughout my body was essential to its proper functioning. Nor did I know I had energy pathways throughout my body that must be *open* for energy to flow freely. Instead, my pathways had become dangerously blocked at an early age. They remained that way for years until this first wave of cleansing, which was one of the first signs of awakening, I've come to believe.

During this time, psychological effects were also unleashed as a whole new "me" was trying to emerge. I say "trying" because I've learned that when we awaken, one of the first things we likely have to deal with are the very people who caused us to shut down. It's not fun, especially when we're not in a condition to fight formidably. That can set up quite a struggle.

When awakening, the body begins to cleanse itself so further energy flow can begin.

My Awakening

Why did I wake up when I did? Because my mother was losing power over me. By the autumn of 2001, she was confined to a bed inside the family home, a log cabin in Wisconsin. After that time, she would never arise from her bed under her own power.

I continue to ask myself this question: How could someone lie in a bed for three years and two months without getting up, without going to the bathroom by herself, and without having her hair washed? Why would someone rely solely on her son to bring her food and change her diapers? All without a doctor's diagnosis?

Yet my mother steadfastly refused help from others. She wanted only her son. As a result, it took her more than three years to accomplish the task of dying while in an environment of poor nutrition, isolation, and relative silence. This could well have been called a suicide, albeit a slow one, with her son abetting the process. He stubbornly refused all help from the outside world—the county, the neighbors, friends, and me. In effect, he helped her die.

I helped, too, in some ways. I needed to save myself from my mother, John, and all of this. So I ran. I had to. A few years earlier, I had started to journal, and all my writing indicated there was trouble that I alone couldn't fix. As I wrote, I knew that others should be called in, but again no one was allowed inside the house. For two years, I did try to improve their situation. Finally, I had to concede failure.

So in 2003, I left to live in Hawaii. Just before I left, John said about Mom, "She borne me; she owes me." This summed up his behavior in many ways.

My daughter, who had just moved to Maui, invited me to stay with her. We both intuitively felt I'd be with her for two to three years, and it proved to be only two. Then, once she left to live on the mainland, I stayed for another two and a half years.

Sometimes it's necessary to remove oneself from a nasty family situation, and geographical distancing can be a powerful ally in healing. Leaving Wisconsin when I did in 2003 allowed me to end the enabling I'd been engaged in with my mother and brother. I can see now I should have left years before, but I would have been leaving too much on the financial table from my father's estate. Instinctively, that was holding me back. (This awareness emerged from my journaling.)

Sometimes it's necessary to remove oneself from a nasty family situation, and geographical distancing can be a powerful ally in healing.

Finally, in 2008, I felt I was safe enough from John that I could return to the mainland. Previously, I knew both the distance and the requirement to cross water would prevent him from coming to find me in his pickup truck.

Being "Nuts" Not the Only Explanation

In reality, both my mother and my brother were "nuts," and what happened in my family was "nuts," to say the least. This is the only rational explanation that we, as a society, recognize today.

However, there's another explanation that can be summarized in one word—*energy*. Not realizing for decades that energy is foundational to everything we think and do caused me to miss this explanation. But as I had one experience after another, I began to slowly process all of my experiences. I've realized they had meaning from the perspective of energy. And I've concluded that recognizing how people abuse both themselves and others is central to understanding life at one of its most fundamental levels, the subconscious part.

To set the stage for what happened, let me describe the home where I grew up.

The family home built by Dad circa 1939

Our Log Cabin in Wisconsin

My brother and I grew up in a log cabin in Wisconsin that our father had built in the late 1930s. Our tri-level half-log home was located near the Illinois/Wisconsin border in Lake Geneva, a favorite vacation town for people living in nearby Chicago. He'd been a builder of log cabins back then and eventually built regular homes, too.

At the lowest level of the house was a basement/garage where Dad parked his Cadillac every night. The next level included the kitchen and a dining room; the latter was used as an office. On the third level was a large living room with an open-beamed ceiling and fieldstone fireplace and "the porch." Each of these levels had at least one outside entrance. Every part of the house could be heated easily except for the porch—originally an open space, but my parents had it enclosed around the time I was born.

Once the porch was enclosed, part of it became a bedroom for my brother, while the rest of it eventually became my mother's bedroom after she moved out of my parents' bedroom—what then became my father's bedroom. I remember the day new furniture arrived and Mom moved from upstairs to the porch. The new bedroom in the porch didn't have heat except through an open door from the living room. I don't think she cared.

Up the stairs were two regular bedrooms (mine and Dad's), the one bathroom, and a balcony overlooking the living room. When I was fifteen, I'd stand and lip-sync to Barbra Streisand music from the balcony, imagining an audience in front of me and feeling free—even if just for a while.

Our rustic house had nearly everything one might think a log cabin would have, including unusual wood doors with handcrafted wood latches and floors that creaked when we walked on them. It had one thing most log cabins don't have though—long wooden dragons along the roofline. Dad grew up in Norway and immigrated when in his twenties. There he would have seen old structures with dragons on them to protect the occupants. I believe it's why he built ours that way. Then he added three spotlights at the eaves on different sides of the house. They were needed to light the yard at night for safety because we lived so far from town.

Aside from not being the usual structure, our log cabin was a regular house. But it's what goes on inside a house that really matters; it's the relationships among the people living there that create the circumstances we react to as children. This house was where my reaction began but not where it ended. It ended

MY REACTION TO TRAUMA   27

The family home 1964

when I finally left Wisconsin and said no to what my mother and brother stood for: favoritism and isolation.

Although I could tell many stories about what went on in that house, the most important one addresses losing pieces of me at the energy level.

MISSING ENERGY PIECES STORY

Four to five pieces of my soul had been lost early on in my life, and I didn't know it. I wish I had known sooner because finally finding them made a huge difference to me. These lost pieces had remained in the log cabin waiting for me to reclaim them decades later.

Let me explain. After Mom died in 2005, I went back to the log cabin to visit my brother three times in 2005 and once in 2006. During one of those visits, I was reunited with my energy pieces. They were waiting for me in the living room at the bottom of the stairs that led up to the two bedrooms.

The first two visits I made were fairly mundane, following the same pattern each time. I flew to Wisconsin from Hawaii and stayed at a friend's house about an hour away from Lake Geneva. After parking my rental car in the driveway, I walked past the outside entrance door to the office and up the small knoll to the next level—to the outside entrance door of the living room. I knocked using the heavy metal door knocker. Even though I had called in advance to let John know I was coming, I had no assurance he would answer the door for me or even be there. But when I said, "It's me," he answered the door every time.

However, from the first moment the door opened, the mood was tense—and that's stating it mildly. My first visit occurred in late July and Mom had died in March. Her estate was still not opened and wouldn't be until the end of August. Meanwhile, John was to inherit everything, including this house and everything in it. Yet, here I was, knocking on *his* door.

Yet even though there was a tension between us, he seemed glad to see me on both visits—perhaps only because I arrived around lunchtime with a bag from Burger King in my hand.

Also on both visits, I sat as near as I could to the front door in a yellow stuffed chair to the immediate left of the entryway. On each visit, I intentionally left the outside door open. Even though it was bright outside when I visited, the living room was dark, very dark. The wood-paneled walls were brown, and John kept the drapes drawn over the windows. I wanted light, so with the door open, the afternoon summertime light poured in.

I also wanted to be able to escape quickly if I needed to.

John sat on a chair about six feet away from me. I stayed between six and eight hours on each visit, sitting on the yellow chair the whole time. I didn't know what to expect from my brother, so I simply let him talk when he wanted to. Still, our conversation was interspersed with long stretches of silence.

Somehow, each visit had its own subject—what *he* wanted to talk about—with the first topic focusing on Mom and the second dealing with business matters. It seemed as if he was downloading information that I might need, depending on how things went later. Although I found it painstakingly difficult to sit and wait for words to come for such long periods, my intuition strongly told me this was necessary—that it would help me in the long run.

When each visit ended, I walked out of the outside entrance door that had remained open the whole time, then got in my car and left. Throughout these visits, we displayed none of the customary emotions one might expect during a visit between the two kids who had grown up together in that house. We simply sat in silence with a few words here and there, while I took notes about whatever subject we were discussing.

But my third visit was quite different from the first two.

Although the third visit started and ended the same way as the others and lasted the customary six to eight hours, this time I had the opportunity to experience something I'll never forget.

I had sought the help of a psychologist months earlier, and the day before this third visit, I had gone to see her. She told me to try to get into each room of the house and just sit there to see what would happen. In each previous visit, only the living room was available to me (except for one quick trip to the bathroom on the third visit). This visit was no different—but it would be enough.

The day of the third visit, I arrived around noon, again with lunch in hand. After John and I sat and talked with the usual silences for about two hours, he suddenly lifted his head and announced he had to make a phone call. He quickly got up from his chair and went downstairs through the kitchen to the office. He didn't own a cell phone, and the landline was downstairs. I heard him close the interior door to the office behind him, but I never heard him dial or speak.

As I sat alone for the first time, my counselor's words came back to me. I stayed seated in the yellow stuffed chair and looked around. Taking a big deep breath, I then allowed whatever was going to happen to do so. In an instant, my eyes (on their own) scanned the room and quickly settled on the first step of the stairs leading upstairs. I "sensed" the presence of something there.

I didn't know what it was, but I felt *joy* emitting from it.

I also sensed it was moving toward me. It took me another moment or two to get the feel of what was quickly coming to me. I couldn't see "them," but I felt the presence of four or five energy forms. It seemed that whatever they were, they were all female, and they were all wearing diapers.

These energy forms each varied in age and development. The oldest one could walk, which meant she was at least two years old. The others were crawling as fast as it seemed they could. The youngest was crawling, too, but moving very slowly. I remained sitting, stunned. I tried not to lose sight of what was happening, as I had no clue this could occur. Then as these forms came closer, I sensed these were all "pieces" of *me* that had somehow been left behind—and now they were coming home.

As the pieces moved toward me, I continued to feel that overwhelming sense of *joy* from them. I had no sense of "what took you so long" or other vibrations of criticism. Instead, I felt their *joy* and their absolute, unwavering conviction that I would come for them—and I did!

Once they reached me, they "leaped" into the energy field that surrounds my physical body. From that moment on, I felt different inside. Later, when I told the counselor what had occurred, she suggested that, as a result of this event, I felt *whole*. Even though I knew she was right, to me I felt *solid,* meaning that I had no more holes.

When my brother came back upstairs, I said nothing about the missing pieces and what had just occurred. He, in turn, didn't speak of the phone call he'd left to make. For another three or four hours, we simply continued as if nothing had ever happened, never shared anything more than the mundane.

Whatever caused my brother to leave the room I'll never know, but I'm eternally grateful for what I learned and reclaimed that day.

What Was the Cause?

What caused this breaking off to happen in the first place? And why did I have *so many* missing pieces?

My best guess comes from a story my aunt told me years later. Aunt Toni was married to my mother's twin brother, Joe. During a visit I made to Florida where they lived, Toni told me about a time in the log cabin when I was quite young. She and my mother were in the living room watching John play with his toys. Toni asked where I was and Mom replied, "She's upstairs in her room." Toni said, "Let's bring her down so she can play, too!" My mother's immediate response was *"No!"* Toni asked why not. "Because I can't put the two of them together in the same room," said my mother. "Johnny gets jealous." Toni then asked, "So, when does Mariane get to come out and play?" Mom said, "When Big John gets home," referring to my father. Unfortunately, Dad generally didn't get home until nighttime.

I didn't know until then that John was jealous of me. Knowing whether it was true or not wasn't crucial. However, it was necessary for me to know that, for whatever reason, Mom wasn't about to put us together in the same room. Even though our family included two children and he was supposed to share toys, parents, and everything else, that wasn't about to happen in *this* family. He was taught he was first. This came from Mom's attitude, and it remained so until she died. John never learned anything different than that from her. Unfortunately, Dad never intervened.

Slow to Walk

If attitude, isolation, and neglect weren't enough, lack of nurturing resulted in my not learning to walk until I was two years old. As a child, I heard the story repeatedly about how I wasn't walking yet at almost two. Mom said she finally took me to a doctor to "see if I was all right." He checked me over and pronounced me fine, saying some children needed extra time and she should give me a chance. I started to walk shortly after that.

This describes the atmosphere growing up in our family home: a jealous brother, a mother who didn't care about having a daughter, and a father who didn't challenge his wife. This statement my mother made about our family dynamics a few years before she died summed it up well: "I had John and Dad had you, and that made everything come out even."

Mariane, Dad, John, and Mom circa 1949

My Chocolate Allergy Story

When I was five, my brother took accordion lessons in Hebron, Illinois, just over the border from where we lived. It was about a twenty-minute drive from the log cabin, so it wasn't far and Mom always drove. I later took accordion lessons, too, but at this point, I was too young.

Often during his lesson, I would spend my time roller skating outside the house where the lessons were given. This neighborhood had sidewalks and we didn't have sidewalks near the log cabin, so this was better than what I was used to. In fact, the only place to roller skate at the log cabin was the concrete floor in the basement/garage where I had to skate in a tight oval. Skating outside with fresh air was considerably better, although I had to watch out for cracks in the sidewalk.

Often after John's lesson, we went to get ice cream at a "ma and pa" place located on one of Hebron's busiest streets. It had a walk-up window so we could order and eat our ice cream while enjoying being outside.

But on one of those trips, my body said *no more chocolate*. As I walked up to the window of the ice cream shop, little did I know this would be the last chocolate I'd eat for *forty-seven years!*

I ordered a chocolate-dipped vanilla ice cream cone and began eating it, then we headed straight for home. Once I got there and walked into my bedroom, my feet had already started to swell. Sitting on the edge of my bed, I had started to put my socks on when I realized something was wrong. I could only get them on up to the arch of my foot!

I bolted for the balcony and went down the stairs calling for Mom. The next thing I knew, she was running to get to the car and I was following right behind her, though I remember it becoming extremely difficult to run. With the swelling, my feet were fast losing their flexibility.

We made it to the car as fast as we could. Because the nearest hospital was forty-five minutes away, our destination had to be the doctor's office only fifteen minutes away in Lake Geneva. I was scared, but Mom drove fast.

I don't recall much except that the swelling kept advancing all over my body. The doctor was particularly worried my throat would close up. Almost every part of my body swelled—my legs, my arms, and even my face—but thankfully not my throat, which remained open the entire time. I remember looking grotesque for at least three days. The doctor gave me medicine alternatively mixed in with either ice cream or applesauce. I never did know what the medicine was for nor did I care.

No one knew exactly what had caused the reaction, but someone decided it must be an allergy to *chocolate* because I could still eat *vanilla* ice cream.

The swelling eventually went down, and I had a lot of bed rest. After that, no more chocolate for me. That meant no sharing in chocolate cake at friends' birthday parties. No more sneaking Hershey bars from the top of the filing cabinet in Dad's office at home.

This state of affairs had lasted forty-seven years.

Almost five decades later, I recall my daughter coming home from college for Christmas break. At the time, I was living in Waukesha, Wisconsin, a suburb of Milwaukee. When she returned to school in Florida, she left a bag of Hershey's Kisses in my kitchen cupboard. During those forty-seven years, I had grown up, graduated from high school and college, maintained a twenty-five-year marriage, had two children, went to law school, and divorced. In all that time, I had never risked tasting chocolate nor did I even think of eating it to find out if my allergy still existed. It didn't seem worth it.

But things were changing.

My Chocolate Release Story

One night in late January 2001 while alone in my apartment, a thought came from out of the blue, meaning from somewhere other than my conscious mind. My intuition said, *I will start to eat chocolate again, and I will be fine.*

"Really?" I responded. "We'll see."

Ten days later, I stood alone in my apartment living room again. It was a cold and miserable February Saturday night in Wisconsin. I *knew* tonight was the night. I went to the kitchen cupboard and got the Hershey's Kisses my daughter had left. I didn't question what I was doing; I obediently followed my intuition.

I opened the half-empty bag and pulled out three Kisses. Then I took them into the living room and sat down on the sofa. Arranging the Kisses in a row, I lit a candle and dimmed the room lights. Then I placed my cell phone beside me and set it to dial 911 just in case. I ceremoniously unwrapped one of the chocolates and put it in my mouth. Smooth and sweet. I liked it. After forty-seven years, how much chocolate would be too much? I didn't know.

Then I waited to see if I'd react. And I waited. Everything seemed okay, so I ate another one and waited again. No reaction. Yea! I saved the last one for the next morning and went to bed unafraid. In the morning, I ate the last one as planned. I still felt okay, or so I thought.

I wanted more! So I began to eat chocolate every day and *felt* I needed to continue for the ten days until Valentine's Day. So I did. Wow, did I! What kind? More Hershey's Kisses, lots of candy bars, Marshall Field's Frango Mints (the best!), and more. I loved them all!

The Crystal Coffin Story

By the following Friday, I had ingested what seemed like a *ton* of chocolate. And because of it, on Friday morning, I had an experience I'll never forget. About seven o'clock in the morning, I woke up in my apartment. As I lay in bed not quite ready to get up, I felt a reaction happening in my feet.

This time I had no swelling, but I felt a numbness moving from my toes up my body—first in my feet, then on to my ankles, then to my legs. It just kept moving up my body. I wondered how far it would go. *What would happen when it got to my lungs and heart?*

The numbness continued to move up and up. When it moved over my lungs and heart, I couldn't hear my heart or hear myself breathe, but I was still alive. The feeling kept going up through my neck and head. I didn't move—and by this time, I couldn't.

It felt like I was in a crystal coffin made of paralyzing energy.

It took only thirty seconds or so for the numbness to cover me. My arms and legs were "frozen" and I still couldn't hear my heart or my breath—yet I was awake. Oddly, only my eyes could move. So I looked around and I lay there waiting for something to change. Nothing did. Scared, I tried to move an arm, a leg, or a finger. No response. *Now I'm in trouble!*

I kept trying and nothing would move. Then *finally* one finger on my left hand responded with a movement that was ever so slight. *But it moved!* I tried harder, and it moved more. That led to the left arm being able to move, and then everything else began to move. The numbness fell away. I leapt out of bed exclaiming, "What the hell was that!" Then I jumped around several times to shake it all off. *Was I okay?* Yes, I seemed to be, but I wasn't sure. So I called my daughter to tell her I thought I'd died. By then, the numbness had gone away completely, and I seemed fine.

Lots of Massages

Having started out in life with a strong faith in God, my intuition naturally developed from the perspective that there was *more*. I've trusted this intuition all my life when I thought to ask. After being in the crystal coffin, my intuition told me I needed massages—lots of them. I'd only had one or two in my life and, right now, I sensed getting one was *imperative*. So I called a place nearby and booked an appointment for that afternoon. I recall telling the masseuse to give me an overall massage, beginning wherever she wanted to.

Intuitively, she started at my feet.

As she came around the table to massage me, I lay in wonder about what had happened to me. Then the *moment* she touched my feet, the biggest tears I'd ever experienced poured from my eyes. After that profound moment, I would never think of massages the same way again.

After she worked on me for an hour, I felt the beginnings of release and relief. Over the next two weeks, I had numerous massages with different people at different locations, each a result of my intuitive guidance. All were needed, though none was as intense as the first one.

In addition to massage, I eventually adopted a full complement of self-care tools that can help people recover from trauma. Please see www.MarianeWeigley.com and click on Resources for a list of healing possibilities for you.

The Restoration Process

This experience also sparked a buying spree the likes of which I'd never experienced before. I bought dozens of items, both for myself and my apartment: makeup, antiques, clothes, new bedding, you name it. With every purchase, I keenly *felt* the word RESTORE coming from deep inside of me. Also, I identified old things from my closets, wardrobe, and rooms and then got rid of them, knowing a massive shift was occurring within me.

I looked around my apartment and could instinctively see that my arrangement of things violated the natural law of energy flow, which some call feng shui. I threw out the cacti from the living room growing in pots—a definite no-no because cacti belong outside a home, not inside. I also threw out the small tree in the bedroom; it was too close to my bed invading my personal space like it was growing out of my head. Out they went!

At the same time, I checked my apartment's directional orientation—a corner apartment facing southwest—to see if I needed to move. My intuition said this was perfect for me. Then I rearranged my bed so my body could soak in as much sunlight in the early morning hours as I lay in bed as long as possible. My bed stayed that way for months. Eventually, I moved it back to a conventional position when my intuition said it was okay to do so.

My ongoing spending grew to thousands of dollars—a lot for me (and probably most people!). Considering I wasn't working full time, paying my bills proved to be a challenge. Although I had to tap into my savings to stay afloat, this strong need to restore myself continued. In fact, my spending put me into debt for the next five and a half years.

Chocolate had started it all, or so I thought.

A Wall of Spices Story

Not long after I started eating chocolate again, I walked into my kitchen and stood in front of the cupboard where I kept my spices. My intuition was telling me to take the spices down from the shelf. I opened the cupboard and removed most of them, but the ones I seemed to want had red and yellow labels—McCormick brand, mostly. The red and yellow colors in the labels seemed to hold a deep significance for me.

As I took each one down, I silently stacked them, one on top of the other, building a wall. *What the heck was I doing?* Yet, I *knew* this was right; I could *feel it* inside. That part of me that had reacted to so many things in the past was clearly at it again. It was proving to be my best friend, as strange as that may sound. But why was I stacking spices this way?

Just before this, I had gone to a Marshall Field's department store (now Macy's) and had bought a cherry-wood silverware chest. Although I'd already purchased the silverware, I hadn't started using it yet, so the pieces were still in the small cardboard boxes they originally came in. I'd never owned a chest for my silverware, and as part of the change initiated by the chocolate, I *felt* it was important for my silverware set to have proper housing.

With the spices now stacked, I got out the recently filled silverware chest and opened it next to the wall of spices I had built. I especially remember noticing how the dinner knives looked in the chest—shiny and new, standing upright in a row looking formidable like weapons—my weapons.

As I looked at the spices and the silverware, I didn't know exactly what was going on. But I *knew for sure* the spices were a wall that, together with the knives, constituted a defense against something—as much of a foe as anything I could ever see. Building this wall was the equivalent of drawing a line in the sand and the knives were a show of force. Doing this felt critically important to me. I was clearly sending a message—but to whom and about what I wasn't sure.

Through this, I was learning about a part of me that can do things on an energy level that goes beyond my ordinary thinking. And even though I couldn't explain this, I could *feel* its significance. This part of me was sending a message—a strong one—in a most fundamental way, making this kind of a wall absolutely necessary.

There could be no mistaking what it meant: *I was going to fight.*

The Role of Intuition

Life happens at the energetic level; what happens at the physical level is a reflection of that energetic vibration. Having gone through what I have, I believe women can lead the way to a better understanding of physical life by using their intuition and self-understanding *energetically*. Perhaps that will reduce the power plays that occur too frequently around us.

Women also need to learn to fight for change using all of their abilities, including intuition. Men have intuition, too, but I believe their ability to access it has been severely suppressed in this culture. A woman I once met said she thought intuition had been bred out of men. Maybe she's right. But I don't believe that's true for all of them. For some, it can be a powerful force, too.

3

The Rules of Energy Flow

*The seen and unseen are intertwined and
one can teach us about the other.*

WORLD EVENTS OFTEN PLAY A SIGNIFICANT ROLE IN how you can discern the way energy can play out in your life. The following story shows how a tragic event carried an essential message I needed to hear at that time. Pay attention to similar opportunities in yours to provide healing insights.

The 9/11 Tragedy Story

I have visions. The weekend before the tragedies of September 11, 2001, happened, I had a vision of people running out of a large head. They ran out of the eyes, the ears, the mouth—any opening available. This "head" represented a structure, but I didn't know what kind or where it was. I didn't realize the significance of the vision either; I simply saw that people were terrified and running for their lives.

My visions tend to come at night or in the early morning hours before I'm fully awake. The evening before this vision of people running out of a head, I was making a beef roast and mashed potatoes for dinner. I had put the roast in the oven, and my intuition told me to give it a good dose of Jack Daniel's whiskey as a kind of a basting, which I did. While the meat was cooking, I made the mashed potatoes and proceeded to mound them into a big heap with a dome shape. I'd never done that before. But I *felt* it was important, so I did it.

Halfway through the roasting time, I *felt* I wanted to put a bit more whiskey over the roast. Never mind that the roast and oven were extremely hot! I added the liquor and closed the oven door. As I turned to take one step, I felt intense heat as the oven door exploded open with a flash of fire.

The fire extinguished itself in a second, with my surprise being the only aftereffect. *What was that all about?* The vision of the large head later that night told me more. However, I didn't realize the two events were related at the time.

It wasn't until the following Tuesday morning (9/11) that these events made horrible sense to me. Then I understood what my intuition was trying to tell me, which is often the case. At home that fateful morning, I had turned on the TV right after the second plane hit the south tower. As I stared at the TV screen, my eyes slowly began to look down and to the side, turning away from the screen involuntarily. This automatic reaction came from a very deep place—not my conscious self. I recall saying: "They did it. They really did it." I had no idea who "they" were, but I *understood* that a part of me *knew* something at a very deep level.

World Events Can Carry Personal Messages

What had happened was indeed a terrible event affecting millions of people. Yet I've since learned that major events covered by the media often convey information to us as individuals about ourselves and our lives. Usually the information is totally unrelated to the event itself, and the need for the information certainly doesn't bring about the act. But the event brings to our attention something we need to know.

For me, the 9/11 tragedy exemplified such an event.

Apparently, I had sensed something significant was going to happen in my own life because I'd signed up for counseling on Monday 9/10—the day before the tragedy. I'd received a postcard from my health insurance provider on the previous Friday saying my insurance would cover counseling. It struck me to sign up for a session right away. I didn't know why, but my intuition told me to act on it.

Several weeks later, I learned my mother was bedridden. About the same time, I saw an interview on TV with a man who lived in New York and rode the subway every day. Speaking of 9/11, the man said he hadn't realized until the towers were gone how big a role they had played in his everyday life. Every time he'd exit the subway and go up to street level, he'd look for the twin towers—that's how he got his bearings.

> *Speaking of 9/11, the man said he hadn't realized until the twin towers were gone how big a role they had played in his everyday life. That was how he got his bearings.*

Hearing this, it hit me. My mother and brother, as dysfunctional as they were, represented *my* twin towers. They dominated my emotional landscape and affected my view of everything. I routinely used them to set my own emotional bearings. Their absence from my life would mean a *huge* adjustment for me. I hadn't known that was coming and didn't know what to do about it. I didn't fully comprehend this until much later on.

USS Greeneville Story

Another example of a public event providing personal information occurred earlier in 2001 when the nuclear submarine *USS Greeneville* performed an emergency surfacing just off the coast of O'ahu, Hawaii. Unfortunately, the sub surfaced underneath a Japanese fishing training vessel, costing the lives of nine people onboard. This happened the morning of my "crystal coffin" experience related earlier. At the time, I'd been eating chocolate again for a week, and my body reacted like that submarine did—that is, it did an emergency surfacing, releasing tremendous energy. The massages I got afterward further supported my body to release built-up energy.

World Events and Energy

How can world events provide information we need to know about ourselves? It isn't crazy. It's real. And here's why.

There's the *physical* side of life as we know it and there's the *energy* side of life. Both make up our daily reality. We tend to think that what we can see is all there is to reality, but there's a lot more. The unseen (energy) side is always creating our physical reality, whether we're aware of it or not. If allowed, it will show us information about ourselves.

A common way it can do this is by what I call "pinging"—a sonar term used by submarines. In sonar, when a signal that's sent out hits an object, it pings off of it, causing another signal to be sent back to the sender. The sender can often tell by the size and shape of the ping what the object is.

When pinging occurs on a personal level, the object you ping off of usually tells you something about you or your life that you have (in some way) asked to know. It can be conveying something totally different than what the object actually is. Often, it's some aspect of the object that, by analogy or even more directly, relates to you and your life. The "object" can be an event, a person, a thing, or a concept—even an odor or scent. Anything. That means whenever you have an inordinate interest in something, assume there may be a deep reason for it. Think of pinging as a form of communication with your deeper self that's reflecting something about You that's essential to know.

Pinging is exactly what happened for me with the 9/11 and *USS Greeneville* events; they "pinged" important information about myself I needed to know. By tuning into your intuition deeply and frequently, pinging will become second nature to you.

The Rules of Energy Flow Affect Everyday Living

Emotions are a major part of the unseen energy side of life that also includes thought, creativity, and imagination. Proper flow of energy inside the body is critical to the proper functioning of this *energy* side of life. Trauma causes energy blockages (dams); so does any emotional baggage we've never dealt with or released.

When blockages exist, they create trouble on our energy side, which then affects our physical reality. Missing pieces—or holes like Swiss cheese in our energy field—cause even worse damage than energy blockages. Why? Because we are meant to be *whole*.

To understand energy and the rules of energy flow, think of your body as a house. The "doors" and "windows" are energetic openings called chakras. The seven major chakras extend from your pelvic region to the top of your head, running front to back. They must be open, and they must spin. You need them. In fact, these energy centers are more You than your right or left arm. If your body has blockages, the chakras don't spin correctly or don't spin at all. If they remain blocked, it spells trouble for you.

While I was growing up, no one talked about the rules of energy flow and their critical role in proper body functioning. My mother, brother, and I all had many energy blockages. My mother and brother likely began developing theirs early in their lives. Their blockages worsened when my dad died, and they continued accumulating more blockages as time wore on. So did I.

My own energy blockages were created early in life, too, but my path was different than theirs. At twelve, I had an epiphany (a thought "out of the blue") that something was wrong in

The Rules of Energy Flow

The following nine rules will help you understand and align yourself with how energy flows.

- Good energy flow can be maintained throughout the body with movement and exercise.
- Energy pathways in the body must be *open* so energy can flow freely. There should be no blockages.
- Energy pathways in the body must be kept *clean* so energy can flow freely. There should be no toxic substances present.
- Energy flow affects your everyday health and longevity.
- Failure to adhere to the rules of energy flow brings on sickness, disease, and premature death.
- Energy flow affects behavior, which is directly related to the level of conductivity occurring inside the body. Setting aside cultural and societal expectations, if the level of conductivity is good, then behavior will be good. If the level of conductivity is poor, then behavior will be poor.
- Energy needs are defined as energy coming in (food, drink, and other things including energy from other people) and energy going out (expended or simply excess being released, e.g., during exercise). These needs, which are unique to the individual, determine and regulate personal energy flow by monitoring what is required at any given time. For example, when you need more of something, you'll seek it; when you have

too much, you'll find a way to either use it up or release it; when you are exhausted, you'll rest to recharge.
- Proper release and flow is the *primary* way to nurture one's wholly integrated self.
- These principles of energy flow are already "known" to each person because they are embedded in the subconscious.

the house. I didn't know what it was. I just knew it wasn't *me*. Believing that message as truth, I subsequently took steps to subtly distance myself from my family. Even back then, I looked to my God for help.

Later, I had a warning about Dad's death. One night as I went to kiss Dad on the cheek before bed, he told me, "My time is near." Even though he hadn't recently been sick, I believed him. I was only sixteen, but I knew what he meant.

Being warned about his death made a difference for me. Neither John nor Mom was in the house when he said that. John was away at college and Mom had broken her left leg skiing. Because of that, she had taken up residence at a house she was building about a mile away on the lake. Even though it was unfinished, the house didn't have stairs to manage while the log cabin did. So it's likely they didn't hear about Dad's premonition.

However, Mom told me after Dad died that she had *known* there would be a death in the family soon. Her intuition alerted her. For example, even though she hated black and never wore it, she had bought a black dress in preparation. She *had felt* it was a male who would die but thought it would be my brother. Instead, it was her husband, my dad, the family's breadwinner. But as a result of Dad's warning, I didn't close up energetically as much as they did when he died of heart disease at age sixty-two. Although his death was difficult for all of us, a safety net seemed to exist for me.

Open vs. Closed Energy

I believe people start life being energetically open, but many close up early on, resulting in a diminished flow that affects their feelings of self-worth. Low self-esteem is just one sign of being energetically closed up. By learning to recognize outward signs, many people can be helped and brought back to being energetically open, experiencing good healthy energy flow and conductivity. This often corrects the disempowerment they suffered due to early experiences. A natural level of self-esteem is restored, and the person gets his or her full power back—even if it's later in life.

The more that emotional blockages disrupt the flow of energy inside, the more dysfunction and disarray will be evident outside.

Besides low self-esteem, symptoms of being energetically closed up include these elements: skin dryness; dehydration; a tolerance and even a preference for a dusty/dirty/musty-smelling environment inside the home; an inordinate acceptance of clutter and garbage. It also can involve a preference for isolation and stagnation, signs of paranoia, dislike of change, and narrow attitudes about life and people. Often, sickness and disease set in early in life. People affected by this often can't hold a job or they show signs of fiscal irresponsibility. They might talk incessantly about the past; for them, there is no present or future.

Again, people's bodies can be compared to a house. When a house is closed up, spiders, insects, dust, and dirt naturally collect. If the house is vacated by its owner, even more damage can happen. Similarly, with a body, if the owner vacates even for a moment due to drugs or other abuse, entities can move in without the owner ever knowing it. If the owner completely vacates, then other residents often move in and take over, just as with any other vacant house.

Generally, the more that emotional blockages disrupt the flow of energy *inside*, the more dysfunction and disarray will be evident *outside*.

A Technique to Use:
Take It Out to the Nth Degree

A lawyer I worked with once said if you want to know the truth of something, extend the circumstances and the timeline out to the nth degree—meaning "to an extreme." Then you'll be able to tell what it is you're dealing with right now.

For example, have you ever noticed how the inside of someone's house reflects who the person is—and even more so when he or she has lived in it for years? Looking for signs of trouble that is brewing isn't easy. You almost have to be a detective or simply know what you are looking for. Signs of energetic dysfunction can start subtly, but then the dysfunction usually grows to be more noticeable—like the inside of someone's house after time has passed. These all reflect what's going on inside people energetically.

Ask this question of yourself: Have you ever noticed something that doesn't seem quite right? You might see it in the houses, cars, possessions, even the behavior of people. Now add a lot of time to worsen the circumstances and imagine what you might see. Extending it to the nth degree in your mind like this will suggest what actions you might take right now.

Perhaps look at the people closest to you—and look at yourself. What do you see?

4

Blockages Start Early On

What might energy blockages look like over time when no one does anything about them?

B<small>Y THE TIME</small> M<small>OM DIED, THE FAMILY'S LOG CABIN</small> house was almost completely closed up, reflecting stagnation inside and out. Weeds replaced the colorful flowerbeds of daffodils, tulips, and poppies that once graced the front yard. The lawn on all sides went unmowed for weeks at a time. Mail and newspapers piled up by the large mailbox next to the road.

In contrast, when I was a child, inside the house smelled of fresh air and, despite the wood-paneled walls, the rooms were filled with light and plenty of it. Back then, most of the drapes were pulled back and the windows open. Fresh flowers from Mom's garden usually brightened the kitchen table. Refreshing!

Our Log Cabin

Because heat naturally rose in the house, the windows in the two upstairs bedrooms (Dad's and mine) were usually open, weather permitting. Being a log cabin, the windows opened in an unusual way. They had wood framing and were hinged on one side. Each window had one big metal hook that coupled with a large metal eye attached to the side of the house to keep it open. As a kid, I knew that once I opened the window, it would stay open until someone came to close it. Absent breezes, we used oil-lubricated table fans in each of the bedrooms to cool us down on summer nights. All the windows had screens during the summer months that were replaced with heavy storm windows screwed on in the fall. The hired men who worked for Dad would do this job.

We used the large stone fireplace in the living room a great deal when I was growing up. Even though we had a furnace in the basement, having a fire in the fireplace helped heat the main living areas and the two bedrooms upstairs. The holidays were never without a crackling fire.

But by the time Mom died, the storm windows were left on most of the windows year-round and the fireplace was cold. Only the windows in the upstairs bedrooms and one of the kitchen windows could be opened. After her death, my brother told me that, years ago, squirrels had started trying to come in through the chimney, so a wire mesh was placed over the top. The house was literally and figuratively closed up.

The only ways to go in or out of this house were through the basement/garage door, the door into the office, and the door into the living room (the one through which I'd enter on my visits). The house had two other doors—the kitchen door and a porch door—but they had been sealed off years before. As a child, I used both of these doors a lot. I liked the kitchen door best because it was the closest to the driveway where my bicycle always waited for me.

Mariane on bicycle, age 6

Just outside that door, a set of flat flagstone steps made a sound when my feet hit them as I ran down them fast. As I recall, the third step always would tip slightly and make a funny "clunk" sound.

The porch door was a favorite, too, in that it led to the backyard swing set and sandbox. I'd play there for hours, alone. Most often, I'd build subdivisions in the sandbox using a small handheld tractor to make the roads, and I'd use twigs for terrace trees along them. After all, that's what my Dad did on a big scale.

I don't know exactly when the two doors were permanently sealed shut. The doors still in use were eventually loaded with multiple locks. In addition, either Mom or John stuck silverware knives in the door jams to prevent anyone from entering.

During the months before Mom died, dust was everywhere and the drapes were drawn, making it dark inside. The furniture severely suffered from the lack of cleaning and the extreme dryness inside the house. My favorite piece in the living room used to be the sofa where I spent many hours watching television or sometimes sitting in front of it on the floor.

The living room circa 1948

We had been one of the first families in the area to get a TV set, first a black-and-white one and then a color set. How amazed I was to see the NBC peacock in color for the first time! Some of my early favorites were *Ding Dong School*, the *Howdy Doody Show*, and later the *Mickey Mouse Club*.

Our sofa, with its two big pillows, was always comfortable and welcoming. Even Panther, our black Labrador retriever, occasionally got to spread out on it. But over the years, the cushions dried out and became stiff. Being on that sofa became like sitting on a piece of hard lumber, the opposite of comfortable and welcoming.

Mealtimes Growing Up

Our family ate meals together in the kitchen, but I didn't get to share in the cooking experience with my mother, who was a good cook. I had to sit on either the bottom step of the stairs just outside the kitchen or on a kitchen stool by the stove just inside the entryway to the kitchen. I'd stay there and watch her make dinner. Right after a meal, she'd wash the dishes and put them back on the table, getting it ready for the next meal. Even though the local 4-H Club taught me basic cooking and sewing skills, my mother had no patience for my helping her with these activities.

During these early years, Dad came home from his office and ate around six o'clock in the evening. John and I had already eaten so he ate alone, with Mom serving him. John and I usually ate when we got off the school bus, around 4:30 p.m. It never seemed to be a priority to have all of us dine together except on Sunday at noon. That day, John and I went to Sunday school and afterward attended the Lutheran service with Dad. Mom never came with us. She only came to church for the Christmas programs put on by the Sunday school.

Usually, the three of us would come home after church and Mom would have a delicious roast beef dinner waiting.

As the years wore on, Mom did less and less cooking. Eventually, the stove stood almost abandoned, and before Mom died, no cooking at all was going on. John didn't know how and adamantly didn't want to learn; he'd say, "It's women's work," as was cleaning. So he used paper plates and the microwave to prepare frozen or canned food. He also never learned his way around a grocery store. The food I saw him prepare for Mom when she was bedridden was meager. He seemed to be thinking that the food would just wind up in her diapers, which *he* had to change. Yet he stubbornly refused to let anyone bring her food or tell him what he should do. Even me. Mom hated change. I, on the other hand, seem to be all about change. Maybe that's why I felt she hated me.

Mom hated change. I, on the other hand, seem to be all about change. Maybe that's why I felt she hated me.

Mom Stuck in Time

Going upstairs to the living room level, I'd walk up the second set of stairs past a progression of photos and my dad's old snow skis to the balcony. Then I'd take a slight turn to the right to reach Mom's bedroom. (After Dad died, she'd moved back into his neat, clean room.) Almost forty years later, when I asked if Dad's clothes were still in the dresser next to her bed, she said they were. I asked permission to check and confirmed it was true. Then I asked about the closet. Were Dad's clothes still in there, too? Yes. Mom was stuck in time.

In another example, when my children were in grade school, they occasionally made artwork for me to give Mom for her refrigerator. When I visited in 2006, those same drawn pictures still hung on the refrigerator. My own "kids" were then twenty-eight and twenty-three!

My old bedroom was a small turn to the left on the balcony level, but John had called it his for the past forty years. Opening the wooden door with its small window, one can immediately see the room isn't very big: a tiny closet, room for a single bed, a dresser, and a desk. Over the years, a few more pieces of furniture had made their way there, along with John's telescope.

Because it's a corner room, it has two sets of windows. I'd sit by those bedroom windows and play my accordion for my grade school classmates who'd come and want to hear me play. Mom never allowed them inside the house, so they had to stand outside my window. This, she said, was the only way I could play for them. They simply weren't let inside except occasionally in the basement/garage area.

My bedroom became my safe haven. I could move my bed to barricade the door shut. (We had latches but no locks.) I could also put a piece of paper over the window in the door, but as I recall, I didn't do that often because the barricade was enough. No one came in to clean except to run the vacuum cleaner over the narrow pathway alongside the bed. And I kept things orderly enough. After all, this was my territory, and I think they knew it. I spent hours there studying for school or listening to music. I always felt safe in my bedroom.

Mom's Car and the Spiders

Mom drove her preferred car, a Buick Park Avenue, for years. It upset her when they stopped making this model; she liked having a car she knew well. With the Park Avenue gone, she bought the LeSabre, a lesser car but similar to the one she liked so much. It was an example of how much she hated change. In fact, she hated change so much, she once said she'd "fight it with all her might." God knows she did. In her car, even changing the clock for daylight saving time proved to be an impossible task. She refused to do it, preferring to always mentally add an hour to the time on the clock.

Then there were the spiders in her car. Sometime before she became bedridden in 2001, I agreed to meet her at a favorite restaurant in nearby Elkhorn. At some point in the visit, she motioned me over to her car to show me something she had for me. I looked in by the driver's side and was astonished at what I saw in the back seat. Cobwebs everywhere! They stood out because the morning sun was shining through the back window of the car. I asked her about them, trying not to sound alarmed. "Could I help clean 'that' up?" I asked. She said no. "They're my friends." I choked back a response and left the issue alone.

Mom's Appearance and Behavior

In the early years, Mom wore dresses, then several years before Dad died, she stopped and switched to wearing casual pants. She never wore a lot of makeup or jewelry, and that didn't change. She and Dad had quite different personalities, but you wouldn't have known it in those early years. Mom knew what he wanted and she delivered. He liked his silk shirts, cufflinks, and suede Stetson hats, his Cadillac, and technology. She, on the other hand, hated technology and liked simple country living and the music to go with it. She would sing "Red River Valley" and enjoyed country singer Loretta Lynn's music, while Dad liked classical music and opera. They were an unlikely couple.

Mom was Dad's second wife (the first being asked to leave after ten years of marriage and no children) and twelve years Dad's junior. Born in November 1914, Mom liked being a Scorpio. She noted that Scorpios are secretive—and she liked her secrets. Dad, born in May 1903, was a Taurus. They most likely came together because Dad wanted children and she was young and attractive.

With essentially only an eighth-grade education, my mother had made her way in the world by being a chameleon and stonewalling people. She kept her head low unless she needed to get something done. Then, look out! All of her smarts

Family portrait taken circa 1952

and drive would kick in. Not a bad trait except when you run right over the people you supposedly love to accomplish what you want.

With that exception, she generally maintained a low profile, kept her friends separate from one another so they wouldn't talk, and made up stories whenever she was so inclined. When I was a child, she would ask me to lie to her friends or others if she didn't want them to know the truth about something.

Before she died, Mom's bedroom became her only room. She lay in one of the two single beds in the room and had a small TV. Because the house had no cable or satellite, the rabbit ears had to do the job of bringing in the one TV station she watched—Channel 10 MPTV, public TV out of Milwaukee. She used a cane to reach out and flip the TV on and off because she had no remote. This, she said, was how she wanted it.

Like my old bedroom, Mom's (formerly Dad's) was a corner room with two windows. The room had the traditional vaulted ceilings of a log cabin, which was how Dad built them. An open beam spanned the ceiling. It was dark like the rest of the wood. For ventilation, one of the windows was generally partially open.

During one of my first visits after she was bedridden, I happened to look up to the ceiling as we were talking. In shock, I saw spider sacks—lots of them—hanging over the other bed as if they were suspended in midair. *Oh God, Oh God. What do I do?* Bringing them to her attention, I told her they had to go. "No," she protested, "they had to stay." John entered the room and agreed with her. "We like them here," he said.

County's Help Not Accepted

In an attempt to get my mother and brother help, early on I asked Walworth County Social Services to intervene. The county sent a packet of information to them, but Mom and John refused all offers of assistance. Eventually, the county sent a nurse to visit, and she got inside to see Mom on three occasions. Each time, she checked Mom's vitals and told both John and my mother what kinds of things they needed to do for her health.

As luck would have it, the nurse was not only a medical practitioner but also a psychiatric nurse. One thing she "prescribed" for Mom was a tablespoon of peanut butter every day to help with brain function. Because my mother liked peanut butter, she generally cooperated with that, at least when I was there. Unfortunately, the county ultimately backed off because John called the nurse's supervisor and said the county was "harassing" them. I later learned from county personnel that this was the worst case of isolation they'd ever seen—and never before with a mother and son. (When it occurs, it usually involves a husband and wife.)

On the third visit to see my brother in the house five months after Mom died, I asked to use the bathroom, which allowed me to walk past Mom's room. I saw that her bed remained unmade as if the ambulance paramedics had just lifted her out of the bed a few hours ago. Next to her bed was a small table that still held a glass of water and a straw beside a jar of peanut butter. Next to the peanut butter jar was a spoon encrusted with dried-up peanut butter.

Mom's Hair

On one of my visits while Mom was alive, I had stayed for several days and slept in the other single bed in her room. Yes, I slept under the spider sacks because my intuition had told me it was the only place in the house I'd be safe from my brother. Having sensed a profound uneasiness about him, to be careful, I honored my intuition.

As Mom had been sitting in a semi-upright position for months, her hair had grown long and matted into a flat bun of sorts in the back. Her body didn't smell, but her hair needed tending to, so I asked her if she wanted me to cut it. She agreed. I found scissors and began snipping away, carefully avoiding pulling any of the tightly matted hairs. After much effort, her nest-like mass finally started to give.

About halfway through the haircut, I had to stop and get out. Ah. Fresh air. I walked quickly downstairs and out into the front yard, almost throwing up. I just kept breathing in the outside air, trying to stay calm. Thankfully, it was a pleasant June day.

When my nausea began to pass, I went back inside. John was nowhere in sight, but I knew he was around. When I got upstairs to Mom's room, I saw she had reached down into the wastebasket by her bed and put the wad of matted, caked hair in her hand. "Mariane!" she exclaimed. "Oh my God, Mariane, I didn't know it was like this. Cut it off! CUT IT OFF!" *That* sounded like the "good" mom I knew. (Like a chameleon, she showed up as two different people—the good one who was there for us on sick days and holidays. Then there was the other mom I walked on eggshells around. On this day, she sounded like my good mom.) I went to work cutting the rest of her hair. Together we got it done, with her participating as much as she could.

Shortly after, I sat down on a chair next to the bed where I slept. That's when John walked into the room.

"How dare you cut her hair?" he barked. "I've been trying to get her to wear a hat so her body heat stays in, but she won't do it. So her long hair makes a hat for her!" I explained to him that I'd asked her, she'd said yes, and that *no one* does what he was describing. He was adamant that "no one will touch her hair until next spring," which was almost a year from then.

"That's not right," I argued. "You haven't even washed her hair! How dare you treat Mom this way?"

He raised his fist, cocked his arm, and muttered, "Why you, son of a bi . . ." As his words began to flow, my instinct kicked in.

I stood up and faced him without flinching, even though I was scared, too. That made him stop mid-sentence.

Mom exclaimed: "Don't fight, you two! Don't fight!"

I saw my moment to get out and walked right past him and out of the room. He stayed still. I don't know what he did next, but he didn't pursue me. This was the first time "the gloves came off" between us. In my legal world, if there are issues within a family, the gloves usually come off when the last parent dies.

Clearly, the gloves were coming off.

Mom's Hoarding

During my visits with Mom after she was bedridden, John never asked me what I wanted to eat, and we never ate together. I'd go to the basement to get a frozen dinner for myself out of the refrigerator with the "good" freezer that was down there. John himself was eating out of tin cans and then leaving them open overnight on the kitchen table. When I told him he could get food poisoning this way and that he should put leftovers in the refrigerator in a different container, he ignored me.

First I'd ask if I could get something to eat and see what Mom wanted, which was always nothing. Then I'd go and get a Healthy Choice dinner and put it in the microwave, which was also in the basement. I always picked out the same dinner—meatloaf with mashed potatoes. To this day, when I'm in a restaurant and I'm grieving, I order meatloaf and mashed potatoes.

The first time I went to the basement, I was astonished to see all the things there—stockpiles of canned goods and paper products including paper plates and napkins that hadn't been there before. Plus the freezer was chock-full. When I got back upstairs, I asked Mom about it all, saying it looked like hoarding. But the moment I brought it up, she said in a hushed voice, "Mariane, I don't know why I did that!" I could tell by the look on her face and the tone of her voice that she really *didn't* know. Yet, it was obvious she knew about the stockpiles she'd created before being bedridden. But why she did it was beyond her.

I think a part of her knew she was losing her grip on life. She also knew John didn't know his way around stores and likely wouldn't go anyway because it was women's work. So I believe she stockpiled so she could just send him downstairs and not to the store. That's my best guess. I know the basement had been messy with clutter and garbage that hadn't been thrown out before, but it was getting infinitely worse. Intuitively, I knew I could do nothing about it.

About John, My Brother

Many of the same things noted about my mother applied to my brother. Like her, in my opinion, he had little or no self-esteem all of his life. He hated authority of any kind. His religion was his own, some form of fundamentalism.

From his appearance during the forty-plus years he lived with Mom, you'd never know he'd had four years of college. And if you saw a photo of him in college, you wouldn't recognize him as the same person. He went from looking like "Joe cool" to a scruffy vagrant. As an adult, although he was never overweight, he often looked unkempt and always wore the same kind of clothing—work pants and a work shirt, or flannel shirts when it was cold. Often, his clothes smelled. The house had a shower in the basement, but he didn't shower a lot.

John had attended St. Olaf College in Northfield, Minnesota, as an economics major. Unfortunately, Dad died the summer before John started his senior year. In his last semester there, he told Mom he wasn't making it in two of his courses. Although he went through graduation for appearance's sake, he didn't actually graduate. Later, he attempted to finish by attending the University of Wisconsin-Whitewater while living with Mom. Apparently the commute of forty-five minutes one way was too much because he dropped out. After that, my children and I were subjected to his diatribes about how bad the education system was in this country and how "they don't teach you anything you can use."

In 1967, John was drafted into the U.S. Army, but while he was stationed at Fort Campbell, Kentucky, he had a thorough medical exam and was sent home, probably because he'd always had issues with his eyesight. I sensed this was a failed opportunity for him to escape Mom on a subconscious level. In the '70s, John was involved in a boating accident that led to one death. Even though he was cleared of any wrongdoing, it left a mark on him. Around the same time, a tenant in one of their apartments committed suicide and John had to do the cleanup. That horrific event also left its mark.

John had a few girlfriends over the years, but they seemed to be as dysfunctional as he was, as far as I could tell. With one, he didn't even tell her his real name—and later I found out when I ran into her at a local store that the name he'd used for her wasn't her real name either!

John Worked for Mom

With the exception of a short time working at a camp for boys in Florida, John had always worked for Mom. He became licensed as a broker in the real estate business Dad started. Mom was licensed as a salesperson, but she basically ran everything. Their business didn't have to obtain property listings because it had enough family-owned inventory to last a lifetime. John maintained the rentals and served as an all-around "go-fer." It seemed as if Mom treated him like a nine-year-old, and he responded by being whatever she wanted him to be.

Maintaining the properties in their business included taking care of the log cabin. As I've described, when Dad built the house, he followed the Norwegian tradition of placing dragons on the rooflines to keep evil spirits away. Unfortunately, a number of years after Dad died, a new roof was put on and the dragons came off. I once asked John where they went. He said that, given the way the new roof was installed, he couldn't figure out how to put them back on.

John in My Old Bedroom

John originally had the second bedroom in the porch next to the one Mom had moved into when Dad was alive. Because that bedroom had no heat and after Dad died and I left for college, he moved into my old room at the top of the stairs. On my visits over the years, I glanced into the room occasionally. It displayed both his lack of tidiness and his reluctance to change things.

In some ways, in fact, he kept the room the way I had it. All my college memorabilia was still on the inside wall, and my college mugs from Augustana College and the University of Wisconsin–Madison were in a corner piece. Also displayed were a few photos of me as a child, plus me at my wedding in 1970. But no pictures in the room reflected a life of his own.

It wasn't until Mom died that I got a chance to check out my old room closely. No organization at all. John had strewn things across the small floor, perhaps because of the limited drawer space. I noticed a shortwave radio he liked to listen to. Other than that, I saw only things of mine I'd left behind. The single bed was my old bed, still with the same mattress I had used decades before. I wondered if my old ponytail hair from seventh grade was still in the dresser.

John's Caregiving

When Mom was first bedridden, I wondered about John's desire and ability to care for her. "Do you really want to do this?" I asked and got an adamant yes.

As time wore on, however, I began to see John had no clue how to take care of her. I hadn't realized how bad off he was. Unfortunately, there was no way to wrestle control away from him without the help of authorities. But they told me they couldn't do much until something bad happened *or* until John or my mother asked for help.

During that time, only a trickle of running water was coming into the log cabin. John's solution? Drive the short distance to the nearby lake in his truck, buckets in hand. He fetched water from the lake rather than fix the water lines that ran from the well in the second garage to the house. Money was not the issue. In fact, it took Mom and me yelling at him together to "fix the damn water pipes" before he finally did anything. The next day after our outburst, a repairman was called in, so at least drinking water became available.

Using the toilet was another issue. Because Mom was wearing diapers and the plumbing in the house was leaking, John told me he was using the backyard as his bathroom. Why fix anything? He saw no problem with his solution.

After Mom died, a good friend of hers told me she'd heard my mother tell John more than once, "You don't ever want to get married." He didn't. Before Mom died, I heard John refer to her several times as his "life partner." He even listened in on her phone calls. When people called, he'd whisper answers to her as a response to questions being asked. Often, his voice could be heard in the background!

John wouldn't let anyone in the house unless *he* wanted it to happen. For example, a neighbor and old friend of Mom's and mine was an emergency medical technician. After Mom died, this neighbor told me he'd tried numerous times to see her once he realized no one saw her driving anymore. But John wouldn't let him in. Also, another neighbor, Mary, sensed something was wrong and called often. On one of my visits to see Mom, John took a call from Mary. She wanted to visit Mom. He went to get her because Mary didn't drive or own a car. He probably did this only because Mom nodded yes since I was there.

When Mary walked into Mom's room and looked around, the first thing she said was, "Bette, why don't you take a handful of pills? It's a whole lot faster." Mom said nothing. Neither did John. But I think Mary called it right. If Mom wanted to commit suicide, pills would have been much faster than what she was doing.

John Didn't Want Me Around

Generally, John referred to Mom as "B," never "Mom." On several of my visits, as I was climbing the stairs to her room, he would yell up the stairs to her, "No one gets your signature, B. No one gets your signature." I had no papers with me and didn't know what he was talking about. I didn't know then that Mom had told him he was inheriting everything and that it was okay with me—which was a lie.

Only when I visited the time before I left for Hawaii did John join Mom and me in her room for any "family" time. He treated me well enough, but I got the sense he was happy to have me leave Wisconsin. After I left, I worried about Mom, but I didn't miss my brother at all.

Several years later, after I became executor of Mom's estate, I began learning more about John. Two neighbors who had lived in the area for years told me John sometimes wore aluminum foil on his chest under his shirt as well as under his hat. Given the statements he made, radiation and aliens seem to have been his issues.

He should have put the dragons back on the roof.

About Me and My Emotional Desert

I had lived in an "emotional desert" almost all my life but didn't recognize it until after my divorce. That's when a good counselor used these words for the first time. Yet I remained numb until sometime after chocolate came back into my life. That's when I saw changes beginning and could understand on a deeper level how the counselor's words rang true.

Specifically, I had married someone like my mother and brother, so my marriage turned out to be a continuation of what I was exposed to growing up. I've since learned this behavior is not uncommon. In addition to the chocolate allergy, there were signs that something was wrong in the house. My mother would talk about having to wake me up to feed me as a baby and it was a fact that I didn't walk until I was at least two.

> **I had lived in an "emotional desert" almost all my life.**

When I was about five, I remember going into my parents' bedroom (they still slept in one room then) and having to go to the bathroom. Even though the bathroom itself was in the next room, I didn't bother trying to get there. Instead, I pulled down my pants and "laid a log" on the carpet next to my mother's side of their double bed. When I was finished, I simply left the room. No one ever said a word to me about it! No "what did you do?" or "go to your room." No response from either of them. Indifference prevailed.

Because there was no day care center or kindergarten in the area, I was sent right to grade school for all-day first grade. Mom had taught me my ABCs and some numbers, so I had no problems academically. But adjusting to school emotionally was another story. Even with recesses, I hated sitting all day at a desk. Other than that, I loved my teacher and I loved not being home. Grade school gave me a refuge and, later, high school provided a welcome sanctuary. Luckily, I did well in school. Education was the one thing Mom approved of, so I learned to use school to my advantage.

Shopping and Living With Mom

Every year in grade school, Mom purchased my school clothes by looking for outfits on mannequins that were all put together, usually including jewelry. She'd ask the store clerk what sizes the outfit came in and then she'd buy all the pieces on the mannequin in my size, jewelry too. We'd go to two or three different stores in downtown Milwaukee repeating the same scenario. I never caught on that she didn't know how to put outfits together herself. However, I remember she'd reject sweaters if the pattern on the front didn't continue on the back because, to her, that meant it was a cheap sweater. (She was right.)

We made these expeditions only once a year—in late August, just before school started. But they weren't fun mother-daughter shopping trips. Rather, I sensed Mom thought it was her duty. As for me, I knew I'd be a prisoner in the car for the whole day, even though for that one day, she could be fairly nice to me. Plus I appreciated getting new clothes that fit, even though I knew they had to last the whole school year.

Mom used to call me a lot of names and once got in my face to tell me I was "UGLY." The way she said it was a long and drawn out "UH—GLEEEE." She looked me right in the eyes as she was saying these words. I *knew* she wasn't talking about my looks; she was referring to "me." I felt devastated. I don't recall ever saying anything back.

For years, I had childhood eczema on the inside of both elbows and suffered from nosebleeds in the winter from the acute dryness in the house. I also had bouts of constipation throughout grade school and high school. My only "relief" came when Mom administered suppositories—sometimes not so gingerly.

Generally, no one in my family paid a lot of attention to me, so as long as I didn't cause a problem—the theme for my life with her—Mom and I got along. But if I did anything she didn't like, she would *yell!* And I never knew when that response was coming.

Having frequently experienced my mother's bullying behavior, at times I bullied other kids. So did John. Since then, I've learned that bullying occurs when someone is energetically closed up and is signaling something is wrong. In response to

> *Bullying occurs when someone is energetically closed up and is signaling something is wrong.* being closed up, people take their frustration and pain out on others, trying to control them in the ways they are being controlled.

My "River Chocolate"

Looking back, by the time I was eighteen, I could see my body had accumulated many energy blockages due to my reaction to the abusiveness in my childhood. Going away to college gave me my first reprieve. There, I could live someplace other than the log cabin with people other than my family.

Yet, I realize now my energy system didn't flow properly, and given that I was missing pieces of myself, the problems my body and psyche were confronting were compounded. In short, I was a mess. If my energy flow had a name, I'd call it the River Chocolate—and that river (like the River Styx) was all dammed up.

The Hell of Being Dammed

Hell is the condition in which you're so blocked (dammed/damned) that you're basically encased in a body that can't function properly. When that occurs, you're cut off from the Universe, from Source. You can't *feel* the way you should, yet the key to your internal steering mechanism and your natural ability to create is your ability to *feel*.

In Greek mythology, the River Styx (pronounced "sticks") separates Earth and the underworld. On the way into Hell and while you're there, you experience the River Styx. The name suggests this river has little or no flow as if it is full of sticks. This analogy resonated for me and perhaps it does for you, too.

5

My Mother's Death

Mom's passing, her funeral, and learning about her estate all reflected who she was. Listening to and following my intuition saved me.

The First Call to Come

MY MOTHER ULTIMATELY DIED IN A NURSING HOME, thank goodness. My daughter and I both feared if she died in the log cabin, John would never call the authorities, and he'd become another Norman Bates (the central character in the novel and movie *Psycho*) talking to his mother's corpse. That was my greatest fear—that is, *before* I saw her will.

Let me go back a bit. Mom had been bedridden since at least November 2001. It wasn't until the first week in January 2005 that John called for an ambulance to take her to the local hospital for treatment. He told me later he called her doctor about a bedsore that wouldn't heal. The doctor hadn't examined her, but John said he'd been instructed to take her straight to the hospital emergency room in Elkhorn.

I pictured what the two of them might have looked like when the ambulance arrived. Mom would have been in a bent position from laying the way she had for so long—fragile and looking like a vagrant, with her hair long and matted again. John probably didn't look much better. He would have been hovering over her as they wheeled her in from the ambulance. He no doubt tried to give the hospital ER staff orders about what she was there for (only a bedsore, he would have said) and declared she should be able to come home that night.

What had actually happened? The authorities confirmed parts of what I'd imagined.

While hospital staff was attempting to treat her, John caused a disruption. Security guards were called in to remove him from the building. On January 13, 2005, he was charged with criminal trespass to a medical facility (eventually reduced to disorderly conduct). Once her son was escorted out of the hospital, Mom wasn't allowed any visitors.

I didn't know she was getting medical treatment until Walworth County officials called me Tuesday, January 11, 2005, to let me know they were filing for temporary guardianship of her person and her property. In the court hearing set for the next day, two female professional guardians from Waukesha were expected to be appointed.

It wasn't until weeks later that I found out John had caused a disruption and was formally charged.

I applauded the county for getting involved. Finally, the cavalry had arrived! Then I asked, "How can I help?" We talked for more than an hour as I answered their questions. I also mentioned a county file had been started on her in 2002 when a nurse had come to the house at my request.

Should I fly to Wisconsin now? My intuition told me *wait, wait* and besides, it would be too long of a flight from Hawaii to get there in time for a hearing. *Should I have someone represent me?* Intuition again said *no.*

After the call, I found it hard to go to work. That morning, I was supposed to see my dentist first thing so I called and moved the appointment to later in the day. Then I paced. *Finally, change was happening. What had taken them so long?*

The official at the county had told me I could call the hospital and speak to Mom, then gave me the number for the nurse's desk by her room. Shaking, I dialed and waited for a ring. When a woman answered, I asked for my mother's room. Someone there answered. After I identified myself, the person put the phone up to Mom's ear. Our conversation was short, but I heard one of the best sounds I'd ever heard . . . my mother's voice. I simply wanted to talk to her.

Her voice came across as weak and showing no emotion at all. I don't recall what she said; it all sounded rather mechanical. However, it was a miracle for me to know she was out of the log cabin and in a safe place where she could get good care. Best of all, I'd be allowed to call her anytime I wanted to.

After that call, all the stored-up emotion inside poured out of me. I sat with my head buried in my hands and cried.

Yes, Go to Wisconsin

I didn't return to Wisconsin until I intuitively got the go-ahead. It was on the weekend of January 22 that I *saw* signs of change and *felt* the *go now* from my intuition. Mom had been transported from the nursing home to the hospital during the middle of a snowstorm that weekend. Thirteen inches of snow had fallen. The nursing home staff said she'd suffered a stroke. Oddly, she was at the hospital only for a few hours, then brought back to the nursing home. When I called, she was resting comfortably, although something had changed for her. For one, the staff said she was very quiet.

An issue of *Time* magazine had come out that weekend and—in another pinging moment—its cover conveyed what was happening. Johnny Carson had passed away, and *Time's* cover headline shouted "Goodbye Johnny." In my emotional world, I understood Mom was saying goodbye to Johnny—*her* Johnny, my brother. Indeed, the Universe told me in a way I couldn't miss—even from Hawaii. When I saw this *Time* cover, I knew what it meant. She was going. So I booked my flight back to the mainland.

I arrived in Milwaukee without a winter jacket or boots. Fortunately, when I'd left Wisconsin in November 2003, I'd stored all my winter clothing in a locker with the rest of my belongings and then turned to a network of awesome friends to help me. One friend gave me a ride to the Enterprise car rental office in Waukesha, about a thirty-minute drive from the airport, with the heat cranked up in the car. I then drove to another friend's house close by. She greeted me with a warm bed to sleep in, food for dinner, a hooded winter coat, and boots for tromping around in the snow. How she got my boot size right I'll never know. The boots were brand-new with a Ross's price sticker on the bottom. Interestingly, there are no Ross stores in Wisconsin, although they can be found in Hawaii and California.

The next day, I drove to the nursing home in Mukwonago about fifteen miles away from where I stayed. Eager to see Mom, I skipped going to my storage locker to get my own winter clothes. Also, I was still fatigued from my overnight flight and didn't want to make any more stops.

Mom had been taken to the nursing home sometime after the first court hearing on January 12, so she'd been there for a while. The personnel were concerned about Mom's safety; they weren't sure about John. He'd been trying to get information about her, but they allowed him to visit her for only limited amounts of time. The visits were never in her room but in a separate room where nursing home staff could observe them both and monitor John's behavior. My kids and I were given passwords for calls or visits; he was not. When I arrived at the home that day, the receptionist asked for my password, to which I replied, "Aloha." She greeted me with a smile.

When I arrived, members of the nursing home staff wanted to meet with me before I saw Mom. They went over a few details, and then we slowly walked toward her room. They'd brought her into a wide hallway area in a movable bed to take her for rehab. We stopped when the personnel with her saw us approaching. "Bette, you have a visitor," one of them said to my mother. Mom looked up and seemed to recognize me. Then she asked, "Is that my Mariane?"

Mom smiled a near-toothless smile. Her eyes and voice seemed happy, but I saw no tears of joy or relief on her face. I leaned down near her face so she could see it was me, and I took her hand. This moment of seeing her daughter wasn't all warm and fuzzy the way a situation like this would normally be, but it was *something* for me. I was filled with relief to finally see my mother.

Mom didn't ask me about Hawaii or the kids. She didn't ask when I got there or how. She didn't ask about John, nor did she say anything about her condition. Nothing. She didn't have much to say about anything. Filling the silent void, the staff and I talked a bit. Because they were taking her for treatment, I said I'd see her later, and they rolled her away.

I then talked at length with one of the administration staff members who brought me up to date on Mom's condition and the situation with John. Neither was good. "She's doing as well as could be expected," I was told.

The next time I saw Mom, she was in her room. Draped over her was a hand-woven blanket depicting the American flag. It seemed unusual but somehow fitting. To me, the American flag represents Soul—something that has kept moving west on this planet to establish freedom. The principles of the United States of America and its Bill of Rights are central to what Soul seeks. Mom's flag told me the Universe was creating conditions that would help to set me free.

Permanent Guardianship Hearing

The Walworth County judge had set another court hearing for February 4 to appoint a permanent guardian for Mom. At the temporary guardianship hearing on January 12, I was told John sat in the back of the courtroom with someone beside him explaining the proceedings. Apparently, people there weren't sure what to expect of him. The hospital personnel had rolled Mom into the courtroom on a bed for the judge to see her for himself. I heard that the first proceedings were tense, and this second was expected to be also. Thankfully, Mom wouldn't be present for this second one.

In the meantime, John had called the previous two temporary guardians "evil" and "sadistic" because they didn't allow her son to see his mother every day. He had canvassed the area looking for an attorney who would represent him at the hearing in hopes he would be made the permanent guardian. He found two. My lawyer later told me the county watched John closely during this hearing to see if he'd do anything that would cause them to get involved with him, too. He didn't. He simply stood there with a lawyer on either side of him and acted civil.

Before the hearing, everyone stood in the hallway waiting to be called in, including John with his two attorneys. I walked in with mine. We exchanged glances, but that was it. I saw no malice and perhaps even a slightly friendly "hello" on John's face, although it might have been a smirk. I wasn't sure.

While we stood in the hall, one of his attorneys approached me and introduced himself. He said he knew who I was, even though we hadn't actually met. It seems we'd argued opposite each other on a case during my time with the IRS in Milwaukee, though I didn't remember him. I knew that was possible, however, because much of my work had been done by mail or over the telephone. He took this opportunity to compliment me on the professional job I'd done on the case. Obviously, I had some credibility with him. *That won't hurt my case.*

After hearing all the parties—John, the county, and my attorney—the judge denied John's request to be Mom's guardian and appointed the person everyone else agreed was a good choice—someone the court was familiar with. Although he was the county coroner, the man appointed also did guardianship work for the court on the side. Because he'd been the coroner for many years, he'd actually met my mother and brother at one of their properties many years earlier when he'd been called to investigate the suicide of one of their tenants. He remembered meeting them both, although he wasn't aware at the time that John was the one who had to clean up the bloody mess.

The coroner's office was in the courthouse next to the sheriff's department. Given my brother's comments to the previous guardians, this guardian seemed like the right man for this job; however, my family's situation would prove to be a challenge even for him.

The coroner wasn't able to attend the hearing, but I got to meet him afterward in a different location. When I first saw him and his car, it struck me how he reminded me of my Dad's style and flash. I thought that similarity would help him manage John from John's viewpoint, but it didn't. In fact, my brother didn't like him, and conversations between the two left the guardian concerned.

The period in the courtroom was the only time I would see John until the day before Mom died in March. Neither of us called the other, and I didn't go near the house. In addition, I made a point of not being anywhere near the nursing home during one of his supervised visits.

Overall, I thought this guardian had done a good job. He seemed to be fair and genuinely cared about the family. I was grateful he hustled to start on the details of this job including paying bills. No one knew everything Mom owned or where it was. And because John didn't help anybody with anything, his job certainly wasn't easy.

Two Weeks of Inner Conflict at the Nursing Home

On most days, Mom seemed happy to see me. During my visits, I fed her and worked with her during rehab therapy sessions. But neither activity went particularly well. She'd say, "Push me," meaning make her do this (be it either to eat or do the exercise), and then she'd stop, as if two sides of her were fighting it out. One side wanted to live; the other didn't. I could only go with whatever was happening at the moment.

Something odd: All my life, my mother had green eyes, but at the nursing home, I noticed her eyes were an almost clear light blue. For some reason, they had changed; I never discovered why. But she was still my mom.

Mom's closet in the nursing home housed lots of clothes I'd

never seen before. The temporary guardians told me she'd arrived with only the clothing on her back, her glasses, and her shoes. They said they had to go out and buy clothes for her because John refused to bring any of her personal belongings from home. In fact, he ignored every request to make her room more familiar and homey. He only instructed the staff to place her shoes on the dresser by the TV set "so she could see them."

During my visit and before returning to Hawaii, my daughter called to talk with Mom. It was a good call—as good as could be expected, although I'm not sure Mom knew who she was. Interestingly, the way Mom ended the call was odd. She said "good night" to her, not "goodbye" or "I love you" or anything else—just "good night."

At That Point We Knew

Right before I left, Mom and I had a "moment" in her room. On this bright afternoon, she was sitting in the special wheelchair ordered for her to make her bent frame more comfortable. With a blanket around her to keep her warm, she seemed content. Then one of the staff members came in, looked at Mom and said, "I'll be right back." When she returned, she brought a small white teddy bear with her and gave it to Mom. In that moment, *I knew* she was going soon. And when Mom saw the bear, I think *she knew, too.*

Shortly after the woman left us, Mom said, "I don't have much time left." That remark gave me the opening to ask about funeral homes.

"Do you want to work with Steinke Funeral Home in Lake Geneva?" It was the one we'd used for Dad, and the owner knew both Dad and Mom. In fact, he belonged to the church Dad, John, and I had attended over the years. I already knew she wanted to be cremated and had left instructions with this funeral home. But I also knew she'd been looking around for a cheaper option before she became bedridden. So I asked if she'd ever found anyone else.

"No," she said.

"So, are you okay with this choice?" I asked.

"Yes," she replied. "It'll be okay."

Safe-Deposit Boxes

In the days that followed, Mom's guardian desperately tried to gather all her bank accounts and other assets to do his job. She had rented six large safe-deposit boxes at her bank. Locating them was easy, but having them opened would prove to be a difficult matter requiring a court order. My brother had the keys at the house and refused to hand them over. When John was informed that the locks would be drilled if the keys weren't turned over, he still didn't respond. Then the guardian and the bank officials notified John exactly when they would have the locks drilled and the safe-deposit boxes opened. The guardian hired a court reporter to attend and record everything found in the six boxes, plus the bank had a representative there to make sure everything was done correctly. John had been told the "when" and "where" so he could be there if he chose to. I later learned it took most of the day—and John did not attend.

Back at the nursing home, hospice was called not long after I left. During the following weeks, hospice staff arranged several phone calls between Mom and me. I appreciated that tremendously, knowing Mom couldn't dial or hold the phone for herself. All the while, I was attempting to work at the law firm that had so graciously allowed me time off when I needed it.

The Second Call to Come

On Monday morning March 14 at 6:20 a.m., my cell phone rang. "Come *now*, Mariane!" the guardian said. "We don't know if she'll make it through the night."

I called the airlines and booked another overnight flight, then called the law office to say I wasn't coming in. As I packed, I phoned John to let him know I was on my way. He was upset about Mom's condition and didn't want me to get upset, too. No real conversation occurred between us except he said he was glad I was coming.

I arrived in Milwaukee about 8:30 a.m. Tuesday morning. This time, my twenty-two-year-old son picked me up. He wanted to come with me to the nursing home to say his goodbye to his grandmother. When we arrived, the staff conveyed to us that Mom was in the "actively dying process" and a woman from hospice was with her.

When I walked into Mom's room with a hospice representative by my side, I saw my mother lying on her back all stretched out. Breathing rapidly, her breaths were also heavy as if she were hiking with a fifty-pound pack on her back. I saw no evidence of pain, but they said she was medicated.

My son had stayed in the hallway until I came out of her room, then he went in alone. He stayed only a few minutes, which is sometimes all it takes to say goodbye. When he came out, he had tears in his eyes and appeared shaken. "That was harder than I thought it would be," he said. I knew what he meant; I was feeling the same.

Right after he left in the morning, the hospice worker and I went back into Mom's room to spend time with her. I remember sitting for hours watching her and talking softly with the kind hospice people.

My brother, John, wasn't there. When he did arrive later around two, the nursing home personnel were willing to relax the restrictions on him that evening so he could stay with her.

Looked at Me With Snake Eyes

From the moment John arrived, the mood in the room was tense. He'd brought a keyboard to play sounds for Mom because he'd learned that hearing is the last sense to go. The hospice worker there—never quite knowing what to expect from him—sat with me quietly in the corner, and we simply watched.

For hours, John sat next to Mom, talked to her, and played the keyboard, pressing one note at a time and holding it. He ignored me and anyone else who came in. Someone suggested he could give me a ride back to Waukesha to the place I was staying. From deep inside, my intuition screamed *NO! Danger.* I could see myself sitting on the passenger side of his pickup truck and him swerving to hit a tree so *my* side would take the impact! Instead, I politely said: "No thanks. Besides, my rental car is already here." Thankfully, by then, the rental company agent had come by with it.

However, John walked with me out to the front entrance of the nursing home. Along the way, he tried to impress on me that *everything* about Mom had to be kept "confidential" and "private." I responded by saying: "It's too late. Other people have been told pieces." He didn't ask who or what but was visibly disturbed that *anybody* knew *anything* about our family and what was going on.

We kept walking. I couldn't reach the front door fast enough. Once we got there, he turned to me and gave me a look I'll *never* forget. His eyelids closed to an abnormal squint; his eyes, like snake eyes, were clearly intended to scare me. He said nothing as he glared at me through the slits.

Breathing a sigh of relief, I gratefully got in the car with the Enterprise rental agent and drove off. Later, I heard that John stayed until eleven or so that evening, after he and Mom had "watched" TV together. The staff said he was quiet the entire time.

The Final Call and the End

The next morning, I got going late because I needed rest and a shower. On my way to the nursing home, I stopped at McDonald's for a burger, fries, and a Shamrock Shake so I'd have something to eat during the afternoon.

The call came just as I was being handed my food at the drive-up window. "How close are you?" asked the female caller. "Get here!" she cried into the phone.

I threw the bag of food on the seat of the car and hit the accelerator pedal. I drove the half-mile to the nursing home as fast as I could. At the same time, I called John on my cell phone and said, "If you want to say goodbye to Mom, you'd better come now!" He responded with "Okay!" and hung up.

The woman who called met me in the nursing home parking lot. She said she couldn't tell me over the phone, but Mom had already gone—about fifteen minutes before. Alone.

It was fitting that she died alone because she'd lived so much of her life alone. And it was fitting I was just on my way, that people on the premises would quickly find her when it was time. All fitting. I hadn't expressed it, but my wish had been that whenever she died, they'd find her right away—that there'd be no Norman Bates problem involving John.

When I walked into Mom's room, the woman from hospice accompanied me. The only light came from the window. Mom lay on the bed stretched out, her face pale and grotesque from the dying process. Her mouth was open and stretched long in a way someone alive can't physically make it do. I took a deep breath and silently sighed with relief at what I saw. She was gone, really gone. *How did I feel about that?*

I stood by her side awhile. Then the hospice lady asked me if I wanted to be alone with her. "Yes, thank you."

I bent down, kissed my mother on the forehead, and said, "Good job, Mom." I knew she'd always been afraid of being sick. In her dying, she'd met her ultimate fear—and conquered it. I couldn't help but tell her I was proud of her. Death had to be an extremely difficult thing for her to face and then allow to happen. Yet it was her time to go and she knew it. The temperature of her forehead was cooling. I said, "Goodbye," and turned away.

Telling John

Next, I had to call my kids and try to reach John. The log cabin phone rang only once before John picked up. Not sure what to say, I told him I had something to tell him. "No. No. Don't tell me!" he commanded. I said his name and said his name again, but he just kept repeating, "No, don't tell me!"

Finally, it was the right moment to say what I had to say. "John, she's gone."

He dropped the phone and started to wail. I heard him pacing throughout the small office in the log cabin, wailing "NOOOOOOOO . . . NOOOOOOOO." The pain I heard in that sound was staggering. Luckily, he didn't hang up the phone, and he never left that room.

Minutes went by. Finally, he came back to the phone. "Do you want to come and see her?" I asked. "I don't know." He wanted time to think, so he asked me to call him back in twenty minutes. I agreed. When I called again, he said he was going to come. "I'll meet you in the parking lot," I offered. "Okay," he replied.

The time went by slowly. I called my children and then the funeral director, telling him to drive slowly because John was driving the forty-five miles to come see her first. Then I sat at a table out in the hallway, not far from the room where she still lay. Sitting alone, I felt grateful for the chance to think and quietly start my own processing.

It also gave me a chance to prepare for meeting John. How would this go? What would he say? What would I say? No way to know. I simply had to trust I'd know how to act. After all, both of our parents were gone and all we had was each other . . . *or did we?*

John Couldn't Go In

We met outside in the warm sunshine and below-freezing March air. We hugged momentarily, then started to talk, but it was awkward. He said he wasn't going to come in to see her. I thought he should, but that it was *his* choice to make, not mine.

As we stood beside his pickup truck, I noticed he brought the one that had mismatched body parts and uneven paint colors. Not his usual green truck, which was in better shape. He brought Mom's old photo album from her younger years. I'd seen it only once—back in 2003 just before I'd left for Hawaii. Before that, I didn't even know it existed.

We didn't look at the album for long. Then as we walked a bit, he kept patting me on the shoulder and back, which he used to do with Mom. Quite frankly, neither of us knew what to do. We talked about finding a church so we could pray, but something made us turn away from that idea and nothing else came to mind. Our drifting apart had become obvious. We finally agreed we'd grieve and mourn in our separate ways.

Within thirty minutes after arriving, John left. He never saw Mom and apparently didn't need to.

Mom's Funeral

Mom used to say, "We have a business to run here, so no funeral and no obituary in the newspaper." Nonsense. I think she just wanted to carry her secrets to the grave. A real funeral would mean a gathering—and that would be an opportunity for people to talk and compare the stories she had told over the years.

She died on a Wednesday with cremation to follow. I was advised by the hospice to have some sort of ceremony—for myself and my children. I took the advice. So on the Sunday that followed her passing, I reserved a room at Interlaken Resort just outside of the city of Lake Geneva on Highway 50. I think the place has been there since the '60s. It needed renovation, but the food would be good and the old-timers would like it, I thought. It had a good feeling about it and a cozy fireplace. The price was right, too. But most of all, it would be private.

I invited my brother, who declined to come. To the best of my knowledge, my brother grieved alone this entire time. The people who did come had known Mom well and for a long time. A few—my daughter, who flew in from Hawaii, my son, and Paulette, a friend from Waukesha—came to support me. My kids were grieving, too. For the first time, they got to meet some of Mom's and my childhood friends. Few of them had ever met my kids.

We shared flowers, stories, and photos. We ate and laughed a bit, but mostly we enjoyed being together. For these people, as well as for my children and me, it was saying goodbye and including others in that goodbye—people who could help us carry the emotional load of secrets she had left us. Actually, we could have used other people to help us carry the life load she burdened us with when she was still alive. Not an option in this family.

Dad's Relatives in Norway

Before the funeral, Dad's relatives in Norway had sent flowers. I asked them if they wanted to attend the memorial, but the trip would take too much time and money. The beautiful floral arrangement the three families sent symbolized their caring for their American relatives. They were missed, but we understood why they couldn't be there.

Mom had traveled to Norway many times since Dad's passing in 1965. My brother had gone four times, too, while my children and I made our first visit in 2001. It took a while for us to go. Mom and John had placed a barrier conveying a message that we shouldn't go. Unspoken but clear, Norway was *their* territory—not ours. But they were wrong. My children and I were a part of Norway as much as they were—and maybe even more. Time would prove we were right.

Dad, the entrepreneur in his family, had come to the United States in his early twenties with a few hundred dollars in his pocket. He did well using his wits and, I suspect, his intuition. My children and I have followed in his footsteps using ours, but my brother headed in a different direction—a direction a lot like Mom's.

Flowers and Friends

The others who came to the gathering brought tulips, hyacinths, and roses, making the room itself look like someone's dining room only with multiple tables. All the tables had white tablecloths. In the fireplace, a blaze was warming the room. The space had a good feel.

The food itself was the home-cooked style we all could relate to. In a way, it was like Mom had cooked it for us all to enjoy. Friends told stories about her that I'd never heard. Some of them I'd known for years and others I'd only met recently, but all were good people worth knowing. All the stories they told were individual ones because they'd never done anything as a group—until now. How odd... like her. Something that stood out for me was that the hospice lady who'd planned to attend didn't show. She's the one who'd strongly suggested the gathering. However, at the last minute, she developed an illness, I was told. I knew that she, as well as others at the nursing home, had had difficult encounters with my brother—perhaps the real reason she didn't come. But John didn't either.

At *exactly* five that evening, the time when the gathering was to begin, my cell phone rang. John was calling to say hello and ask a not-so-important question. He said he'd forgotten all about the gathering. I asked once more if he was coming. He declined but wished us well.

Road Trip to Spread Her Ashes

There would be no burial for Mom. Instead, the following Wednesday, my children, John, and I planned to spread her ashes. Mom wanted cremation "so the worms wouldn't get her," she had told me. And she wanted the ashes spread on a cemetery plot in southern Illinois near the old house she grew up in, which meant a six-hour trip for us. No talk about a will or finances at this time; we had a scattering to do.

We rented an SUV for the trip and offered John a seat. At first he declined, but the next day—the day we were to leave—he called to accept. He told me he hadn't been more than one hour's driving time away from home *in years.*

Even though his place was an hour out of our way, we swung by to get him. Leaving after my son finished work made it already dark by the time we picked up John to start out. We had a long way to go.

Although my Dad is buried in a plot in Lake Geneva, Mom had a gravesite prepared for herself close to the grave of her father in southern Illinois—far away from her husband's grave in southern Wisconsin. The gravesite had originally belonged to Grandmother, but Mom had it transferred to herself. She always said she wanted to be buried next to her father, her only friend. Interestingly, Grandmother is buried in a plot near my father's in Lake Geneva.

John got in the SUV dressed in his usual worn dark-colored parka and blue jeans. He toted a plastic milk jug filled with water to drink. Oh, yes. He smelled, which wasn't unusual. He asked to sit in the front seat because he gets carsick. (I'd forgotten about that; he'd been that way since he was a child.) So we let him sit in the front.

The ride went well except for some nasty weather. I drove most of the way but turned the wheel over to my daughter during the snowy, icy part. I was getting exhausted by the strain of it all. About one in the morning, we arrived at the hotel in Belleville. We'd reserved two double beds and one rollaway for the four of us. Even though we offered John a bed, he slept on the floor in his clothes under a blanket. He never said why he chose that. It was clear from most of his actions that night he didn't feel comfortable around us, yet he wanted to be with us.

In the morning, we missed the free breakfast the hotel offered because we all slept in. Astonished to learn that some hotels offer free breakfast, he spent time asking questions of the hotel staff what we'd missed.

Then we set out to find the cemetery. I'd been there before so I knew the way, but I wasn't sure where to go within the cemetery itself. Once we got near it, we stopped for food at a Denny's before we went looking for Mom's gravesite. John loved the menu there and the busyness of the place. Here, too, he was overly amazed at the variety of food. He ate up and so did we without engaging in much conversation before going on our way.

Finding the Plot

On this cold, sunny day, finding the right plot wasn't easy. We had to be secretive because we were pretty sure spreading ashes on a gravesite was a no-no according to cemetery rules. Mom had asked that we spread most of her ashes on the grass of her grave and then spread some of her ashes on her father's. Both had headstones but not side by side. Mom's plot was located one row and several plots from his—the closest she could get, she'd once told me.

There, we opened up the back of the SUV where we had placed her ashes and some of the flowers from the Sunday dinner. The box, made of a white-colored cardboard, was relatively heavy and had the name of the crematory on it. I was able to pick up the box out of the car and take it over to her plot. Standing right by her headstone, I opened the cellophane bag inside. The ashes were smooth except for occasional chunks that looked like broken seashells washed up on ocean beaches. I knew better. They were bone fragments that hadn't completely disintegrated during the cremation. Disregarding the cold, we left the lid on the back of the SUV open the whole time. Because the mood was tense, leaving it open somehow gave us a sense of purpose and urgency.

As we were about to start scattering the ashes, John asked if he could have some of the ashes to take back with him to sprinkle around the outside of the log cabin. We agreed to hold some back in the original bag and give it to him to take home. He appreciated it.

Not an Easy Task

Sprinkling her ashes wasn't easy in the cold wind. We stood silently around the gravesites—hers and Grandfather's—as we scattered them. The ashes blew. We then selected a few of the flowers and laid them on each of the graves. My kids and I hugged each other (I don't recall if John was included in the hugs) and took photos. All the while, we looked out for the cemetery staff; we didn't want to get busted. Yes, we were just carrying out our mother's wishes, but sometimes the law doesn't care about that. Luckily, no one approached us.

Just as I spread the last of the ashes and we paused, I looked to the right, and right above the trees in the not too far distance, I saw two Canadian geese taking flight. They climbed up over the trees and then made a big circle around us and the gravesites. It was as if Mom and her father were now united, taking flight together for the first time since he'd passed so many years before.

She was where she wanted to be.

The modest event took maybe an hour. We left the cemetery as we arrived—in silence. Looking back, I realized that neither of us had brought our own flowers to put on either of the graves.

It was a full year later when I thought to ask John what happened to the ashes we gave him. He said he'd locked them in the trunk of her Buick and they were still there. To me, locking them inside the trunk of her car was either revenge or the best he could do—and maybe it was some of both. *Fitting.*

6

Closing Her Estate

One thing I've learned is that trusting your gut raises issues efficiently. That's because trusting your gut is all about trusting You.

WHAT A MESSY AND DIFFICULT ESTATE! MY MOTHER had committed fraud against my brother and me, and it only came to light at her death. She got away with it.

To be specific, during the administration of my father's estate (in 1965), Mom breached her fiduciary duty as executor. In his will, my father had named a bank president as the executor of his estate, and he had two law firms ready to handle everything. However, three years into it, all of them resigned. The court then gave Mom control as administrator *de bonis non* (basically executor or personal representative). This event was the game changer for John and me back then. With this control, she could then steer things the way she wanted. And ultimately, John and I would be worse off because of it.

Dad's will instructed that two trusts—one for John and one for me—were to be set up on our behalf, each funded with 25 percent of the assets. But Mom was the one who got all of the assets. That's embezzlement. And that event resulted in a completely different life for me and for John.

Further, Mom also had John sign an Assignment, giving the assets he was to get under Dad's will to her. That was both illegal and a breach of her fiduciary duty. As a result, all of his assets from Dad ended up in Mom's estate later when she died in 2005. When we tried to get John's assets out of her estate, we were unsuccessful because of the Assignment. Because the assets were in Mom's estate, they were subject to state and federal estate taxes, costing John a sizable amount of money when they never should have been in Mom's estate to begin with. Mine either. But there was no such Assignment affecting my assets so we were able to get them out of her estate without suffering loss due to estate taxes.

Evidence of Embezzlement

When the IRS first saw the issues involved in Mom's estate, they wanted to charge her (that is, her estate) with embezzlement. The IRS claimed that the embezzlement occurred when she stood before the court as executor in July 1976 and stated that John and I both received what we were entitled to under my father's will. A lie. And she knew it. She *knew* she'd manipulated John, and she *knew* I hadn't signed anything. John and I did not have our own legal counsel to represent us back then, and the cause of action of breach of fiduciary duty wasn't as well developed as it has become.

After Dad died, the court didn't appoint a guardian for John as he was so close to age twenty-one, but because I was only sixteen, a guardian *was* appointed for me. However, that guardianship ended when I turned twenty-one. To this day, I've never met the lawyer appointed to watch over me regarding this estate during that time. I'm certain my mother ran interference to make sure that no one, especially a lawyer, ever talked to me to inform me (or John, for that matter) of our legal rights. Although we would eventually both receive what Dad wanted us to have at Mom's death, it was forty-seven years late.

In the end, John received substantially less than I did because his share had to pay estate taxes due to the Assignment he'd signed. However, Mom left him other assets that were transferred directly to him at her death. The combination of the two inheritances would secure his financial future.

Mom's will stated John would be the executor and, if he couldn't serve, then I would be the executor. This is the same will that was giving him virtually everything, and if he wasn't alive, it all went to *his* children (if he had any, which he didn't). *Only if he was gone and had no children would I inherit anything.*

Who Would Be Executor?

During the times John and I spoke at the house, I saw John move his head from side to side saying nothing but displaying uncertainty. Then he'd quickly turn, look directly at me, and say I should be the executor of Mom's will because it needed my kind of "brain power." Even though he had four years of college, which might have helped him, I have to admit he would have been in over his head. Given the complexity of the situation, I was in over mine.

Eventually, after we individually filed a claim against her estate for 25 percent of the assets, the judge appointed *both* of us to be co-special administrators. A deadline was then set for us to resolve who was going to be the executor because, in this case, there should be only one.

A special administrator doesn't have the full set of powers an executor or personal representative does. This meant first we had to agree on the claims and whether the estate would recognize them or not. In fact, this matter didn't get resolved for another eight months. Finally, at the eleventh hour, a resolution was reached. Earlier, John had called me in Hawaii almost three months after Mom died and said, "I know I have to do something." He was referring to the 25 percent Dad wanted me to have. Now, Mom's will said it was all going to him.

In that phone call, he further said he didn't know what he was going to do. Here, almost a year later, I was receiving a fax of an Agreement drafted by his lawyer stating John agreed to not object to my claim if I would not object to his claim. In general, it said I would be the executor, but I'd have to pay 25 percent of all the estate administration legal fees and reimburse John 25 percent of the statutory fees I'd be paid as executor. It also stated I had to waive the small bequest in the will—one thing that Mom had left me except for a bank CD that passed directly to me outside the will.

I won the fight to be the executor or personal representative, but my dignity took a hit. Even though John agreed, he did so only upon facing a deadline set by a judge who said if there was no agreement between us by that date, he would have the case administered by people outside the family. That was when John agreed to do "something"—at least, I believe it came down to that because I never heard him say he *wanted* to sign something. It was always couched as something he *had* to do.

I can also say being the executor of an estate that involves family when you're *not* a named beneficiary felt *horrible, demoralizing, and embarrassing*. But what could I do? In the end, I persevered.

Described as "Difficult"

Even though we found forty years of accounting records to prove neither of us had ever received any assets, having John involved in this estate presented difficulties. As adults, it was time to grow up. For the most part, people seemed to be on my side because they saw how "difficult" he could be—at least, that was the word I heard most when others described my brother.

When we were first appointed co-special administrators of the estate, the estate lawyers and I suspected if something required his participation, nothing would get done. As a result, we set up as many procedures and methods as possible that didn't require his signature or his direct approval. For example, when the estate checking account was first established, the bank cooperated fully by allowing only one signature to be required when signing checks. (Customarily, two signatures would have been required.) When I first arrived to set up the account with almost six months of deposits in my hands, they seemed to understand the problem. They said when they'd seen Mom and John together at the bank in the past, they witnessed behavior that had raised issues for them. So, as I was opening the estate checking account, the bank official turned and asked, "How many signatures?" She could see by the documentation that two administrators for this estate had been named. So she asked: "How many actually need to sign the checks? One? Two?" I looked at her and repeated what the estate lawyers and I had resolved to do, concluding by saying, "Only one signature would be needed."

She looked at me calmly and paused. Then she turned back to the computer screen and said, "I think we can do that." The estate finally had an active checking account so I could begin to pay the bills that had been unpaid for more than five months.

Looking back, timing was important. I sensed when to get to the bank and which branch. If I'd gone to any other branch where an employee might have done it "by the book," the outcome needed—namely, one signature instead of two—might not have happened. But because this bank official had some history with Mom and John, it worked out.

Trusting Myself as a Form of Energy

I've learned that having an understanding of me as a form of energy is a critical component to trusting my gut. Being ready to trust those nudges I feel deep inside is a proper response—for me or anyone—because it acknowledges me as a being made of energy. *Without* that understanding, I'd be at a disadvantage when dealing with life issues. *With* that understanding, the advantage is mine.

I knew getting the estate opened would require using my intuition and trusting my gut in a way that would prove to be critically important. For example, early in the process shortly after Mom died, I called John's lawyer whom I'd heard had just been fired. As I was driving (while in Wisconsin), I felt a sudden sense of urgency to pull over, park my car, and call this lawyer. I did. He took my call. After he confirmed he was no longer John's attorney, we talked. I gave him my side of the matter at hand.

Interestingly, within a few minutes, his secretary informed him that John was on the other line waiting to talk to him. That ended our conversation, but he now had information he'd never get from John. Eventually, John hired and then fired him again and later hired an attorney from Elkhorn who would ultimately be his attorney throughout the estate administration. As will be explained shortly, making this change proved to be fortuitous for my claim on this estate in the long run, and I believe neither one of them ever realized it.

Essential Visits

All of my visits to the log cabin in late July and early August that first year gave me much-needed information. I instinctively followed the nudges I felt about when I should go, what I should bring, when I should arrive, where I should sit, what I should say, when I should stay silent, and when I should leave. All of these gut-driven responses helped bring about a miracle each time. For example, it was at the log cabin that John gave me both information and insight I'd need for the estate administration. Plus it was there my missing pieces returned to me—pieces I didn't even know were missing. *That,* especially, was a miracle, and it made me stronger.

In fact, getting information from John at any other time was impossible. He ignored phone calls and generally didn't respond to his mail. In one of our sessions, he told me he'd only go out at night because he didn't like sunlight. Odd. His snake-like eyes and drapes pulled shut secretively told me *something* was going on.

Being "Difficult" Continues

During one of my visits, John confessed to accidentally throwing out numerous rent checks he had placed in a black garbage bag for safekeeping until they could be deposited. Further, he told me the names of the tenants, how much they paid, and who was up to date and who wasn't. None of this was written anywhere for me to retrieve. I usually brought paper with me on these visits, but I seemed to never have brought enough. I certainly didn't know what to expect each time I went. But not having enough paper was only one of the problems I experienced. When I get nervous, it's hard for me to think straight, so I wrote down whatever I could on whatever I had with me.

Still, John kept making it impossible to get things done.

"Mariane, you don't need a lawyer," my brother said right to my face as we stood in his attorney's office in late August, a full five months after Mom's death. (Estates are usually opened within a short time after the death.) I have since learned when someone says, "You don't need a lawyer," that means you *do* need a lawyer! John had learned from Mom how to stonewall and bully, so if one of these two methods didn't work, then he'd do the other. This pattern showed up every so often during the administration of her estate, especially at times when he didn't like what was going on.

Just before this, we'd been sitting in the conference room where the mood was so tense, it could be cut with a knife. John's lawyer had placed my mother's guardian at one end of the table next to me and one of my lawyers, and, opposite of us, himself. When my brother first walked in with his lawyer, the lawyer sat John down at the opposite end of the long conference table so he wouldn't be near any of us. I was grateful for that. But John would be facing the guardian, and that could mean trouble.

As soon as John's lawyer sat down, we began going through the large box the guardian had brought with him. The box contained the contents of Mom's six large safe-deposit boxes that had been in his possession since they'd been opened in March. Because the estate had been officially opened by the court the day before, the guardian could turn them over to me and John as co-special administrators.

Bills Piled Up

As we went through all the items to be covered, one matter stood out. Bills had been piling up since March and needed to be paid. One bill in particular needed to be paid first relating to the property tax bills that hadn't been paid by my brother in July. The guardian had taken it upon himself to pay the bills that added into the thousands! Because he didn't want the taxes to go into arrears, he found a way to pay them out of his own pocket. The fact that he was owed this money briefly came up when he handed me other outstanding bills: for the ambulance, the hospital, the nursing home as well as electric bills and gas bills for the house and the apartments. My brother hadn't even *tried* to pay them, even though he knew they were accruing.

After discussing the bills, we'd moved on to a new subject when I stopped the conversation and brought it back to what the guardian had done. I looked straight at my brother's attorney and said: "I want you to know something. I don't think you realize what this man did for our family. He paid thousands of dollars *of his own money* to cover our property tax bills because John (my brother) refused."

John's lawyer stared at me, then looked at the guardian who was finally getting his due for this generous act. The lawyer then glanced irritatingly at his client sitting at the end of the long table. That's when I saw something I'll never forget. The air around the lawyer's body turned a translucent brown—an ashen color. It surrounded his head and shoulders, and extended down his body. I could still see what was behind him, but this stunned me. His emotions were emitting this ashen color *and I could see it. I could read my brother's attorney! Oh my God!*

How important would this be? Only time would tell.

Strong Negative Emotions

I had seen auras before, but not like this and certainly not in a legal situation. So I acted as if nothing had happened, but I knew that, for this to be occurring, my brother's lawyer had to be feeling strong, negative emotions about what was coming to light. He turned to the guardian and sincerely expressed his appreciation for what he had done. Indeed, the first check I wrote was the reimbursement check to this gentleman—in full.

When the time came to pay the first property tax bills in December, the estate ran into trouble again. It didn't have enough money to pay the tax bills. The money we had in the estate was used to pay Mom's final bills, while the rest went toward paying the looming state and federal estate tax bills that were due—and they were *big!*

At this point, John and I, as co-administrators of the estate, had a problem. We needed to liquidate assets, and my brother's signature was required for that. As a result, we had to file a petition with the court for an emergency hearing requesting that my brother be removed as co-special administrator. Thankfully, the night before the hearing and with a court deadline looming, John agreed to be removed on his own accord. That meant we could start liquidating assets and begin to pay all the other bills that were quickly accruing.

The Energy War: Mom, John, and Me

If I thought Mom was a problem, John was worse. But I always thought I stood a chance with him. Specifically, I was fighting everything she'd taught him about women—attitudes that were awful, cruel, isolating, and disempowering. Their attitudes had subjected me to an entirely different life than I could have had.

> *Standing up for oneself against one's own family members has to be one of the most difficult things an individual can ever be expected to do.*

Standing up for oneself against one's own family members has to be one of the most difficult things an individual can ever be expected to do.

Resolving Mom's estate proved to be my moment to stand up for myself. I'd never taken on Mom directly—or John, for that matter. I should have. This represented the eleventh hour to fight or die (at least financially). It took courage I didn't know I had and required a lot of help, which somehow showed up.

When I'd moved to Hawaii, in addition to the state's natural energy, I felt a sense of empowerment simply by leaving Wisconsin and distancing myself from Mom and John. Once I was there, I *felt* I would be successful at some level regarding this estate. In addition, my own finances weren't in good shape, so I had nothing to lose by fighting.

I want to stress the importance of my living in Hawaii at the time and not being anywhere near John. Without Mom, I was next in line to be an enabler to him, but I wasn't going to be there to do it. That would push him energetically, and it probably wouldn't be a pretty sight. He'd naturally begin to grow emotionally and mentally again without me there, and I doubted he would like it much.

Between Mom's death and her will, I felt it was like experiencing the grand finale of a fireworks display. The biggest and loudest (and, for me, the worst) were saved for the end.

When the Grand Finale Started

The beginning of this grand finale actually started in 1984 when my husband, my two children, and I moved to Lake Geneva—a place I swore I'd never return to. However, it *felt* right at the time. There wasn't much professional work there, so I did volunteer work and also became a property tax assessor for a local township. I wanted to do more—but what?

So at the end of 1986, I asked a longtime friend what she thought. She told me frankly, "Mariane, I always thought you'd end up in politics." That career had never occurred to me. Then one day I found myself watching C-SPAN on my TV in the kitchen. Later, I became aware that a high percentage of people in Congress are lawyers. Still, no whistles and bells went off. But just a few days after that, I *heard* what I needed to hear: *I needed to go to law school in order to become the person I always could have been.*

That statement blew me away. I'd never even thought of going on to school. It had been fifteen years since my undergraduate degree and, besides, I was married with two children. The only law schools near me—and luckily there were two—were in Madison (University of Wisconsin) and Milwaukee (Marquette University).

Finding a Law School

I started looking into law schools in January 1987. Luckily, I called Madison first. The person I spoke with told me the school had a part-time program, but it was called "extended time" because of an American Bar Association rule that a student could take no more than six years to finish the degree, with the norm being three. I made an appointment to meet with someone in admissions.

Driving the one and a half hours to Madison, I kept repeating out loud as I drove: *"I can't do this. I'm married with two children. What am I thinking?!"* But something kept me going.

Actually, I'd once lived in Madison for ten years, earned my undergraduate degree there, and had my first child there, so I knew the city and university campus fairly well. After parking in a familiar parking ramp near campus, I walked up Bascom Hill. In all my years of living, working, and going to school in Madison, I'd never stepped into the law school building—until that day when I walked in, scared and overwhelmed. *I'm in over my head!*

Before long, I sat down with an admissions counselor who answered all of my questions. I can recall getting up, walking out of her office after a half hour or so, and going out into the hallway. I stopped. I looked around. *I knew I belonged there.*

Then I drove all the way back to Lake Geneva in contemplative silence, feeling truly stunned.

At home, I said nothing to my husband or children or anyone else about this. A few weeks later, I called Marquette University Law School and asked about its part-time program. This time, I didn't use the phrase "part time." Instead, I said "extended time." I found out that was a critical difference. Marquette had recently begun its extended-time program and didn't want people to think of it as part time. But because I used the correct phrase "extended time," I was told about the program and its rules, how to apply using the normal application procedures, and then how to request extended-time status.

Again, I set an appointment to meet with the admissions counselor. The entire hour it took to drive there, I repeated the same things to myself I'd said on the way to Madison. I didn't know Milwaukee very well, but I found the campus, parked, and walked into the law school building, taking a deep breath. The history and energy of the building itself were enough to make me pause.

My meeting with the admissions counselor was like the one at Madison—lots of questions and answers. From this meeting, I was able to receive the information I needed. Again, when I left the office and stood in the hallway, I *felt* the same thing—*I belong here.* Clearly, I had to apply.

During that time, the ratio of those applicants admitted to Marquette's law school was only one in seven. Thankfully, I was among those accepted in 1988. We bought a house near Milwaukee close to where my husband's employer was located. From our home there, I had a forty-five-minute commute to campus.

While at Marquette, I thankfully received scholarship money and picked up a few awards, including membership in the Law Review and an award for the Federal Income Taxation course I took. I was even given an appellate court internship for a semester.

I took out student loans (which my husband willingly co-signed) to get me through the program. It ultimately took four years to complete. Mom and John paid nothing toward my law degree, nor did they ever contribute one dime toward buying our house, despite what I later heard she'd told her CPA. And sadly, my husband provided no help regarding my family-of-origin issues. In fact, he was actually part of the problem. For example, he saw and heard negative things about me from my mother but never acted on them in my defense. Because I didn't need any more of his disregard, I divorced him within four years after finishing law school. In retrospect, I realized I had married the kind of person I was used to with Mom and John—someone who was emotionally distant.

First Job After Law School

After graduating from law school, I worked in a medium-sized law firm in Milwaukee. Without any assistance at home, it was tough working full time, dealing with a forty-five-minute commute, and still getting the work done at home I was expected to do. Without the support I needed, the firm and I parted ways after almost two years. Fortunately, this led to a better job at the Milwaukee IRS office in the estate and gift tax program. (Due to the program's sophistication, the IRS hires only attorneys.)

This job proved to be a godsend right from the first week. I was sent to Atlanta for four weeks of intensive training in estate and gift tax along with two other attorneys hired for Milwaukee and thirty-seven more hired for around the country. There, I met an instructor and attorney who later became a personal and professional supporter in my family estate matters. This was 1994. Mom wouldn't die until 2005, but here I was, already positioning myself for a Big Fight that I wasn't even aware of! I was a lawyer who was now gaining tax knowledge and coming into contact with people who could handle the sophistication of the problem I'd encounter many years later.

In the course of the four weeks in Atlanta, I made friends and experienced a feeling of "family" that had never existed before. For this, I was truly grateful.

"Fortunes"

In 1998, I began to travel for fun, which we hadn't done during our marriage. First I took a cruise with my daughter, and one of the stops was Jamaica. There, while riding in a tourist van to see a local waterfall, the first of many "fortunes" (like those in fortune cookies) came my way.

We had stopped at the falls, got out for a few hours to enjoy the beauty, then returned to the van. I was the first of the group to return. The van had been locked and so were the windows, but I could see a slip of paper on my seat—and only on mine. When I got in, I picked it up and read, "You will have many friends when you need them."

Later, during the time I was with the IRS in Milwaukee, I had the good *fortune* to have many cases with the local attorneys who specialized in estate planning. Long after I left that job and after Mom died, one of my law school friends offered to ask one of these attorneys to take a look at *my* case. After reviewing what I had, he agreed to take the case. This attorney did a fabulous job representing me, and ultimately, this case became a life changer for me and my children.

Working with my former IRS instructor, these two attorneys performed a miracle. By filing a timely claim against my mother's estate for the full amount owed to me under my dad's 1965 will, they raised an issue that my mother and brother thought was long gone. Specifically, I had not received my share from Dad, and any reports to the contrary were proven wrong by the court documents and the forty years of accounting records that Mom's CPA found archived at his firm. It was the CPA who pushed to find them, if they still existed. The actual claim was filed by one of my local attorneys. (Another attorney for me in Oconomowoc, Wisconsin, handled many aspects of the case as well.)

My Legal Cavalry

Even though I was a lawyer, I couldn't have done this all by myself. I was too close to the case and didn't have the experience I would have needed. Thankfully, with his twenty-eight years of estate and gift tax experience, the now-retired IRS attorney was a tremendous help, giving us critical advice when we needed it.

In effect, that advice reinforced what we already knew, but it gave me confidence to keep going. Specifically, he told me to file a claim against the estate within the legal timeframe and make it for cash. We might have won John's claim for him, too, except the Assignment Mom had him sign in 1976 was in place.

Having the right kind of legal power behind me proved to be crucial. Trusting my gut and following the nudge to go to law school at age forty began the process of making the friends and connections I'd need in this fight down the road. There, I met caring attorneys who had the expertise, sophistication, and credentials to work this case.

Becoming an attorney myself and getting hired by the IRS added to my credibility, which helped me deal with the legal community I was up against in Walworth County. Learning estate and gift tax law directly from the IRS mostly gave me a knowledge base, allowing me not only to understand the technical aspects of the case but also participate in discussions. Because I was the executor and the case was so unusual and personal, having this understanding proved helpful. It also didn't hurt that I had not only reviewed estate tax returns while working for the IRS, but I had also prepared them while working at the law firm in Hawaii.

All of this background gave me incredible insights I could apply to my own case. The defensive "show of force" I'd experienced in 2001 when I stacked the spices and pulled out the silverware chest had foreshadowed this whole experience.

The Outcome of the Estate

I knew Mom's estate would eventually close, but I didn't know how or when. True to form, in the estate's last months, John refused to agree to the final accounting. Unfortunately, his signature was required. Once more, litigation loomed—a delay that would likely add another two years!

When the court set a hearing date for why the estate was having trouble closing, I *knew* I had to be in Wisconsin. I realized the court only needed me to "appear" by telephone; I'd done that before from Hawaii, and I could do it again now from California. But something told me I had to be present in Wisconsin—not in Walworth County per se, but in the area—and being in Milwaukee would do.

I hadn't been back to Wisconsin in two years because there had been no need until now. I also *knew* I was *not* to set foot in Walworth County. I didn't know where that message was coming from or why, but I knew I should respect it, so I did.

I flew to Wisconsin on Saturday, September 24, 2011, but as it turned out, not to attend a hearing. It was no longer needed. At the request of John's lawyer, we had sent one more settlement offer to him prior to the hearing date. The following Monday, one week before that date, we received word that John had signed it. So while in the area, I signed papers and deeds and transferred bank accounts in accordance with the final settlement.

Equitable Distribution of Assets

As we were trying to close the estate in 2011, I kept "hearing" the phrase *land for John and cash for Mariane*. I knew that wouldn't work because there was more land than cash at the end. But who was I "picking up"? For the most part, I thought it came from my brother. But eventually, I realized it was from his lawyer, and with that realization, I changed. When I discussed the situation with an attorney friend in California, she gave me the words I needed by saying, "What you're looking for is an equitable distribution." I hadn't thought of putting it that way, but that was true enough. So the very next time I "heard" a voice saying *land for John and cash for Mariane*, I fired back mentally with the thought: *No. An equitable distribution is what I want.*

At that point, the estate matters shifted and shortly after, we reached a resolution. Finding the right words and mentally transmitting them back (which I hadn't done until then) proved to be the game changer that led to the resolution I was seeking.

As I sat signing the real estate deeds according to the settlement, I experienced a moment—*the* moment. I had just finished signing John's deeds transferring estate land to him. Then it was my turn. Sitting in the conference room alone, I paused before signing the deed that would transfer land to me in my own individual right. I *knew* this was the moment I'd been fighting for. By receiving family land, in essence, I was being recognized as part of my own family—finally. *What a moment of deep satisfaction.*

Settling the estate took an extraordinary amount of time. Partly, this was because it had one federal estate tax audit (never fun), one federal income tax audit (no picnic either), two claims against the estate (difficult because it meant arguing for them with the IRS), and a lot of real estate to be liquidated in a tough real estate market. Luckily, I had visions and telepathic transmissions too numerous to mention that all helped bring about a favorable outcome for me and my two children.

What a week of floating on air! It took weeks, months, to process that the tension of uncertainty I'd lived under for almost seven years—the entire time of this estate administration—was over. It also meant that after sixty-four years of being in this dysfunctional family and doing my best to be loving, I could be free (although I've learned that decompression is a necessary phase after a major event like this, so I expect processing it will take years).

Was the Fight Worth It?

Monetarily, was this fight worthwhile? No one could have guessed Mom was worth several million when she died. My 25 percent share became a portion of that, counting part of the interest I was also able to acquire. The estate didn't have enough in assets to pay John and me our claims in full plus interest, and therefore we had to prorate how much each of us would receive. Yes, the fight was worth it. *I am grateful.*

But to a certain extent, no amount of money would ever be enough to compensate me for the losses I'd experienced over the last sixty-four years. At the same time, no amount of money could ever buy the things I learned. Plus, until this point, I don't think anyone had ever pushed John the way these proceedings did. All those years, Mom knew how to control him. She taught him how to bully and stonewall to get whatever they wanted from each other and from other people. And it all came to an end at her death.

Being executor, I could clearly see this during the estate dealings. In the end, John and I were left with no relationship with each other. I might say Mom didn't care about relationships being built, but I don't know that for sure. I do know she herself never fostered deep ones. Why I don't know, but I have an idea. I think she had experienced dissociation as a child as well.

Sharing My Story to Help Others

Finished! I had won. I feel John had won, too. He now has plenty of resources to last his lifetime. He now has his freedom from a mother who "got it wrong" and freedom to live as he, himself, wishes—something he's never had. I don't know if John knows what to do with his freedom, but I know what to do with mine—*live!* Live as authentically as I can at this point

> *At a deep level, I know that sharing my story will empower others. I've felt this for more than a decade—even back in 2001 when I was stacking the spices and lining up the knives in the silverware chest.*

and help others. At a deep level, I know that sharing my story will empower others. I've felt this for more than a decade—even back in 2001 when I was stacking the spices and lining up the knives in the silverware chest.

7

Restoring the Flow

After having experienced trauma, it became critically important for me to adopt new ways of living in balance and expressing myself fully.

After my mother's death, settling her estate, and getting on with my life, I needed to turn my attention to my own health.

Growing up, I did the bare minimum people do for their health, namely annual visits to the doctor and dentist. I finally experienced my first massage when I was about fifty, which became part of my awakening described earlier. The release from my chocolate "allergy" came right around the corner at age fifty-two. A lot of self-care has followed.

Some people know they're in a bad situation and *stay* in it likely because they fear facing the unknown. But I never even asked questions to find out how bad my situation was—not with my family members nor in my marriage. In fact, the thought *never even entered my consciousness.*

It wasn't a matter of *choosing* to stay in these relationships; I had always operated on autopilot. Before I even realized big issues had been looming over me for years, it was incredibly easy to shut me down or shut me up. How could I not see the pattern in its entirety? I couldn't; it was simply too close.

Finally, Standing Up for Myself

Part of my healing was learning to stand up for myself and claim what was rightfully mine. It took me forty-seven years after Dad died to acquire the inheritance due to me. (Other than my dad, longevity seemed to run in our family, so I couldn't simply wait for John to pass after Mom died.) Why did it take me so long to pursue what was rightfully mine?

Because nothing could happen until Mom passed, I spent the last twenty-four years of those forty-seven years raising my children, going to law school, paying off student loans, divorcing my husband of twenty-five years, and trying to help Mom as her life energy dwindled. But when I found that *nothing had changed or would change* in my family, I left Wisconsin and went to Hawaii to live with my

Why did it take me so long to pursue what was rightfully mine?

daughter for almost two years. Luckily, I found a good job in a law firm with great people. Yet I still experienced stress, depression, poor finances, and deteriorating health.

As mentioned earlier, the IRS rehired me. When that happened, I even got a pay raise. Eventually, the IRS changed its retirement system in a way that allowed me to retire three years earlier than I expected to. As another bonus due to retiring from a federal job, I now receive health insurance for life. Because I don't know what long-term effects this entire deeply stressful experience will have on my health, I'm mighty grateful to have this coverage. I can sleep peacefully knowing I'll have help when I need it.

Doors Open for You

Learning how you *should* be treated is the first step in understanding how abuse and energy relate to each other. Chances are you won't know exactly what I'm talking about until you go through similar changes and feel the difference for yourself. It's incredible what can happen:

Doors begin to open for you; new doors you thought were closed to you.

You feel the Universe is moving *with* you instead of *against* you.

Aligning with "All That Is" becomes your norm.

My Healing Process and My Health Today

Guided by intuition, I frequently wrote in my journal, meditated, and did picture puzzles to help me heal. Throughout this nightmare with my mother and brother, I had trusted my intuition to tell me what to do, what to say, whom to say it to, and when to say it. I *felt* when to make necessary phone calls and whom to see to get things done. For example, all the visits to my brother at the log cabin in 2005 and 2006 were orchestrated this way, from deep within. Timing proved to be everything. Without the third visit and reclaiming my missing parts, I simply wouldn't be in the position to tell my story, raise significant health issues, and open a discussion about human energy.

Today, my emotional numbness is generally gone, and my life is being restored. It feels like *a grand old ship is righting itself after being pushed over onto one side and left to rot*. I'm ready to set sail and see what I can accomplish, even this late in life. For me—and for you—it's never too late to right your own ship.

I gradually began to wake up and heal by releasing blockages, experiencing the process of energetic change, and both discovering and incorporating my missing pieces. Not all people have pieces missing, but my sense is that many do.

Over time, I also incorporated life-balancing components using various methods. Once my blockages began releasing, I discovered how it's critically important to adopt new ways of living in balance and expressing myself fully. No more holding back.

> *For me—and for you—it's never too late to right your own ship.*

(On my website at www.MarianeWeigley.com, I share ways I've learned to count on to release blockages and/or stay balanced. Click on Resources.)

Experiences like mine encompass many types of abuse: withholding, enabling, neglect, and isolation, which resulted in dissociation, a form of psychological numbing and disengagement. These can cause people to shut down; some even die from them.

A Resolve for the Future

As children and people, we can become like the unwanted toys that ended up on an island in the Christmas story about Rudolph the Red-Nosed Reindeer. Some were broken, some had missing parts, and all were damaged in some way.

Many people shut down the way I did because of how they were treated early in life. Most won't have the resources that I did, but shutting down is shutting down, and that is what causes the damage. It's a profound reaction. And it is a natural reaction to ensure survival. But it creates significant problems later.

I hope to reach as many of these people as I can and offer them much of what helped me. Then maybe they, too, can become the individuals they could have been *except for those early experiences that caused them to shut down energetic*ally.

Abuse like I experienced on any scale should not be tolerated, because it's wrong. It's abuse that uses energy to cause disempowerment and ultimately leads to a diminished life experience. Anything else than full empowerment is not acceptable. It goes against Universal Law, which dictates that every soul, every individual, be treated with respect.

Restoring is about bringing You with your energy system back to life. Given the time spent dealing with Mom's estate, I've been twelve-plus years in the restoration phase. I suspect the process will continue as I keep growing and developing. Abuse like I experienced on any scale should not be tolerated, because it's wrong. It's abuse that uses energy to cause disempowerment and ultimately leads to a diminished life experience. Anything else than full empowerment is not acceptable. It goes against Universal Law, which dictates that every soul, every individual, be treated with respect.

8

The 60/40 Split

*Trusting my intuition helped me learn how
I experienced dissociation.*

What is dissociation? What does it look like?

THE STORIES I SHARE HERE ARE MEANT TO PROVIDE an instructional reference and even a mirror for healing dissociation. As you read them, be open to recognizing similarities in your own experiences.

The Iceberg Story

In May of 2001, a few months after my chocolate release, I had a feeling something wanted to surface into my consciousness. I'd been restless and didn't know why. I felt this surfacing was going to be different, *really different*. I had a super busy weekend ahead of me and I sensed that whatever this was would take time to rise slowly rather than pop into my head. I needed to plan for it. *Sunday, late afternoon, would work.*

That Sunday afternoon around five o'clock, I sat down at a table in my living room next to the sliding glass door that led to the balcony outside. Then I placed a pad of paper and a pen in front of me and gave myself permission to sit and wait. My second-floor apartment faced south and west so it always had a lot of light and because it was May, the sun hadn't set yet. I had turned off the TV and radio and could hear only a few sounds outside. I simply sat and looked off into the distance. *What could be so important for me to feel like this?*

I just waited. It took a while and finally something stirred inside. I *knew* that feeling. Something was coming up from the deep; it headed straight for my head and my consciousness. Slowly, I could feel my brain trying to grasp something. It would try and then I'd lose the piece I had. *It felt like nothing I'd ever experienced before—like an iceberg surfacing.*

I could feel my brain trying to wrap itself around something, but this was so big, it was having a hard time doing it. About thirty minutes passed, and then "it" came up. As I sat in the chair, my lips formed five words I will remember forever: "I missed the whole thing."

At first, I said these words without feeling, although I knew exactly what they meant. Then I cried out, "Oh, my God, I missed my whole life!" I stood up and jumped up and down, shaking my right hand. "I missed my twenties, my thirties, my forties, and here I am fifty-two, and I've missed the whole thing! I missed all of it! Oh, my God!"

In shock, I paced from the living room to the bedroom back and forth like a caged wild animal. I couldn't believe it, yet I knew it was true. Yes, I had a marriage; yes, I had two great children; yes, I went to law school. But I was not "all there" for *any* of it. The better part of me was hiding or just plain somewhere else. *I missed the whole thing!*

Another thirty minutes passed and finally I could sit down. With those five simple words—*I missed the whole thing*—my life changed. How could I look at anything the same way anymore?

It took weeks for the meaning of this event to fully sink in. First, I grieved and mourned my loss—the loss of what could have been. I was grateful for all I had, but that didn't help the deep feelings I experienced. After grieving for months, finally, I began to ask myself deep-seated questions. Most important of all, I asked, "What do I do now?"

Dissociation robs people of time, and I had lost most of my life to it.

The Second Apartment Story

To save money, in 2002, I moved to a new apartment with a low rent that included utilities—a godsend. It was the lower level of a split-level home owned by the daughter of a friend. I had one bedroom, one bathroom, and a large central living area. Its good-sized windows in the front and in the bedroom gave me enough light, even though the apartment faced north and east. I shared the kitchen upstairs and was given one cabinet for my kitchen things and a designated area in the refrigerator. I was allowed to use the laundry, which was on my level, but from time to time, the owner would also come down and walk through my living area to get to it. She was wonderfully accommodating to me, but it was still a difficult adjustment. I'd recently left the privacy of my apartment where I'd lived for seven years—where the chocolate release had "happened" and where I realized I'd *missed my whole life*.

Shortly after moving, I remember walking into my new space and confronting a war zone of boxes and things strewn everywhere. Turning to the left at the bottom of the stairs toward the living room, I stopped in my tracks, stunned. To one part of me, everything appeared just as I had left it earlier in the day. I recognized every item and could tell you where I bought it, when I bought it, how I used it, and more.

At the same time, another part of me looked around and didn't recognize *anything*. That part of me had never seen these possessions before! It seemed like my vision had a 50/50 split—with one eye seeing it one way and the other eye seeing it the other way. Blinking my eyes didn't change anything; I just stood there astonished.

But I didn't panic. Actually, I acknowledged that this strange sense had been building since my chocolate release twenty months before. Although I'd noticed some aspects earlier, I was now experiencing a dramatic, pronounced change.

I've realized that dissociation caused by trauma creates odd occurrences like this. Later, I realized it was more of a 60/40 split than 50/50. What followed was a process of integration in which both parts slowly learned to operate as one. That was the good news. The bad news was that basically all of my life experiences—my marriage, my children, and most of my education—was imbedded in the 40 percent part, while the 60 percent part had to learn almost everything new. For some reason, driving a car was not a problem. Maybe this was because I learned how to drive *before* Dad died. Just a theory...

Since then, I've had to stop and routinely ask myself, "How do I want to do this?" Indeed, much of what I did certainly didn't come automatically the way it used to. Yes, the 40 percent was comfortable in its patterns, but the 60 percent changed all those patterns.

"What Is My Community?" Story

When I was forty-nine, a few years before my chocolate release at age fifty-two, I experienced a foreshadowing about a big change coming. It started with my counselor asking me, "What is your community?" I replied, "I know what you mean, but I don't know the answer." It took me almost a year of processing all the other things we talked about before I could respond to that question. But when I did, it took me only a few minutes.

One day while living in my first apartment in Waukesha, Wisconsin, I deliberately sat down with a pen and a piece of paper and I asked the counselor's question: "What is my community?" I already knew I didn't have one because I just didn't *feel* one. So digging deep, I asked these questions: "Is it Waukesha?" *No,* came the answer from inside. "Is it the Milwaukee metropolitan area?" *No.* I broadened the question. "Is it the United States of America?" *No*—and before I could even finish saying the "United States of America," I *knew* the answer because I could *feel* it. It was the *whole world*, including the Universe.

I was amazed I had a community at all, but I was especially taken aback to realize how big it actually was. I took it all in, and I've never looked back.

Later, I realized I'd gone from having no community to belonging to a community that's everywhere and includes everyone on the planet and beyond. *The barrier that had blocked my sense of belonging had dissolved.*

Over time, I've learned that dissociation causes a kind of detachment that makes people feel they don't belong anywhere. What was happening? It was a sign that the dissociation was beginning to break down.

Two Picnic Table Conversations Story

Before Mom became bedridden, she and I had two conversations about the money from Dad. In the summer of 2000, we sat at an old wooden picnic table in the backyard of the log cabin. On this warm, sunny day, we had plenty of shade from the trees. Although we didn't use the picnic table much over the years, we did from time to time. But these times were never the happy kind imagined when a grandmother, uncle, daughter, son-in-law, and two grandchildren gather. That's never how this "family" operated. On this visit, Mom and I were the only ones.

As we sat, she raised the subject of where her will was located for "when the time comes" and added, "Johnny doesn't want to hear anything about it." I already knew the place because she'd told me before—that is, in her safe-deposit box at the local bank she liked. It was tied with a red ribbon, she said. Not new information. But she had never discussed what was in her will (and I'd never asked)—until now.

Looking away without showing emotion of any kind, she nonchalantly continued, "I just want you to know that I'm leaving everything to Johnny, and that there's a little something for you." I was dumbfounded. I had no idea she was planning this!

Feeling hurt, I reacted with silence. I simply looked at her and she continued to look out over the backyard. Not once did she glance my way. *I said nothing. I had no words to say. I was speechless and hurt.* Then we just sat there and went on like nothing had been said.

Remarkably, a whole year later, Mom and I were back at the same picnic table on another summer day. This time, I brought up the subject of her will, saying, "Mom, remember what you told me about how you're leaving everything to John and there's just a little something for me?"

Without facing me, she said, "Yes." She continued looking out over the yard as she'd done before. I then found the courage to articulate what I'd been holding in for a whole year: "Mom, then I don't have anything from Dad . . ." I said slowly. My eyes were steeled on her, looking for a sign that "this" (meaning she was leaving basically everything to John) wouldn't happen. No such sign came. Instead, she paused and without breaking her gaze toward the yard, she said in a wistful way, "I know . . . but I don't know what we can do about that." Then silence.

Again, I had no more words to say. As before, the conversation ended, and we both acted as if nothing had been said about the will. It took a long time for the word *betrayal* to even enter my consciousness.

Dissociation does this, too. It results in silence. Looking back, I can't believe this happened to me. *I simply had no voice.*

How Dissociation Works

I had shut down at an early age in order to protect myself. The shutdown part became "frozen" or wasn't even there at all. Chocolate and time helped to make the 60 percent "thaw." Reuniting with my missing pieces was part of this scenario as well.

Unlike many, I'm one of the lucky ones to have come out of it. Experiencing the iceberg coming up, realizing the 60/40 split, and gaining a sense of community were all signs I was coming back—restoring myself. Counselors told me I'd eventually be okay.

WebMD.com defines dissociation as "a person's unconscious attempt at self-protection against an overwhelming and traumatic experience. . . . The mind separates itself from an event or the environment so it can maintain some degree of order and sense."[1] In a severe form, a dissociative identity disorder (previously known as multiple personality disorder) can happen.[2] Dissociative disorders can happen even without the occurrence of overt physical or sexual abuse.[3] They can appear in families in which parents are "frightening and unpredictable."[4]

Even though I never had blackouts or was mentally missing periods of time (which can occur), "frightening and unpredictable" aptly describes the log cabin environment I grew up in. What happens in environments like this can speak volumes years later.

1. "Dissociation," by Healthwise Staff, accessed November 14, 2014, http://www.webmd.com/hw-popup/dissociation.
2. "Mental Health Center: Dissociative Identity Disorder (Multiple Personality Disorder)" reviewed by Joseph Goldberg, MD, on May 31, 2014, http://www.webmd.com/mental-health/dissociative-identity-disorder-multiple-personality-disorder.
3. Ibid., 4, http://www.webmd.com/mental-health/dissociative-identity-disorder-multiple-personality-disorder?page=4.
4. Ibid.

Dad's Funeral in 1965 Story

Dad's funeral was held on Friday, June 18, 1965. That's when I learned Dad had been married before. The morning of his funeral, Mom asked me to drive into Lake Geneva to meet some people from Chicago at a restaurant parking lot so I could lead them to the church. "Who are these people?" I asked. "Relatives of your dad's first wife," was her answer. "What!?" I said. She gave me no explanation, just a "get going."

I went, met them, and led them to the church—mission accomplished.

After the services and the cemetery burial, the mourners met at the house that Dad had used as an office. People brought food and filled the place with chatter, as was customary. But what happened in the receiving line shook me. Mom, John, and I lined up inside the door in front of the fireplace—Mom first, then John, and then me. We all greeted people as they came in. But what happened next repeated itself often. Mourners would come in, speak kind words of condolence to Mom and John, and then they'd turn to me, pause, and politely ask, "And who are you?" After this occurred a number of times, I got the message. These people hadn't met me, nor I them. Yet, they all seemed to know John and Mom.

"Mariane, Give Johnny the Toy" Story

Years later, about 1999, I was sitting in a restaurant in Waukesha having lunch with a new friend who knew spiritual matters well. In particular, she had a knack for helping people lift out old memories.

By chance, we began talking about my mother and something stirred deep inside. I began looking straight into my friend's face and, without my uttering a word, she stopped the conversation and said to me, "I think I can hear your mother's voice." Then, with that simple prompting, I heard *both* my friend's voice *and* my mother's voice (in my head) saying *exactly* the same thing at *exactly* the same moment. Those words were, "Mariane, give Johnny the toy."

> *I didn't know memories could get stuck inside, let alone be lifted out years later.*

I could only imagine what must have occurred so long ago! I suspect we were likely in the living room of the log cabin and I was forced to give a toy of mine to him. I didn't know memories could get stuck inside, let alone be lifted out years later.

Before the sentence even finished, huge tears came to my eyes and ran down my face—just as they did during my first massage after my chocolate release. I felt so relieved, I broke down right there with lots of people around. I didn't care; I couldn't hold back the strong swell of emotion. Mom hadn't died yet; she wasn't even sick (that I knew of). I also didn't yet know about her will. I just cried as I relived this moment from childhood.

Afterward I felt better, though sad and infinitely grateful it happened—like having a thorn removed that had been festering for years.

My friend had helped to lift that big, awful moment right out of me.

Afterward I felt better, though sad and infinitely grateful it happened—like having a thorn removed that had been festering for years. I've come to learn that huge tears like I experienced are powerful releases from the deepest levels inside. They represent traumatic events and moments of great pain held at those levels for years and ultimately causing, in my case, dissociation. Tears to the soul (as in something being ripped) result in actual tears (as in crying).

9

The Four Abuses Explained

*Deep inside, it felt as if someone (Mom)
let go of my hand way too soon.
It was like an absence, a silence, a hole that
no one else (but Mom) could fill.*

COMING OUT OF DISSOCIATION IS A STEP-BY-STEP process. These stories shed light on what it was like for me. How might they be similar to your own stories?

Emotional Numbness Story

In early 2003, I had a chance to talk to Mom and John on the phone. I was living in my second apartment in Waukesha, while they were forty-five minutes away in Lake Geneva in the log cabin. At this point, Mom had been bedridden for more than a year, with not much being done for her. The house had two phones, one of them positioned by her bed.

Both Mom and John were on the call. At some point in the conversation, I finally broke loose and said things I should have said years ago. With my left hand holding the phone away from my head, I yelled into it, "Whatever happened to this family?!" They had no defense or answers. *Had I even gotten through to them that something was terribly wrong?*

I said this several times more, once even jumping up and down as I screamed into the phone. *Still nothing!* So I slammed down the phone, disconnecting them. To their credit, they called back. We went another round—questions from them and questions from me. But I could see I wasn't getting through, so I hung up again.

They called back one more time. We spoke further, then finally we all agreed to hang up and talk later—sometime. Shortly after I'd hung up, my eyes were involuntarily drawn to the palm of my left hand. They actually stared at it. Then something strange began happening that I didn't initiate nor try to stop. I knew myself well enough by then to allow events like these to unfold by themselves. I felt my left hand tremble and shake and then *really* shake. After that came the *pain*—a *horrible pain* like the kind you get by slamming your hand with a hammer and you know the pain is coming, but because it's so extreme—off-the-charts painful—it doesn't come right away. And when it does, it's *excruciating!*

I jumped and screamed in anguish. *The pain just kept coming.* But I had no hammer—only a telephone receiver.

Only later did I realize those words I needed to say had been stifled for years. *Oh my God, it took how long?* Truthfully, the time between suffering the emotional experiences and feeling the pain from them took *decades.*

In between, I was, to a great extent, emotionally numb.

Discovering WENID Story

What factors had led me to dissociate? Through my journaling I was able to pinpoint four of them: Withholding, Enabling, Neglect, and Isolation. In 2012 I saw how they led to Dissociation. I refer to these factors collectively as WENID.

In my case, withholding, enabling, neglect, and isolation are all forms of *emotional*, not physical, abuse. No one slammed me against a wall, burned me with cigarettes, or scalded me with hot water. But emotional abuse is equally as damaging as these physical acts. Why? Because without visible scars, no one knows the severe hurt that's being inflicted deep within. When what I experienced happens in a household (or elsewhere), the aftereffects may stay with the child, even as an adult.

During those decades of numbness, I survived by becoming heavily analytical—hence a lawyer, and a tax lawyer at that. I didn't know heavy thinking could be a coping mechanism, but it was in my case. Being highly intuitive also helped me survive.

In my journaling in 2001, a part of me identified these four abuses as being the ones I'd been most subjected to. Since that time, I could always say them quickly, one after the other, until it got closer to putting them down on paper for others to read. Then I'd stumble when I tried to say the list. I'd always forget one—but never the same one. Odd.

That led me to finally sit down and, analytically, create an acronym of the abuses so I'd never forget them when asked. Settling in with paper and pen, I began to play with the five words: dissociation, withholding, neglect, enabling, and isolation. *What would be the correct acronym for this?* It didn't take long for that deep part of me to kick in with the answer after I let my hand go wherever it wanted to go on the page.

I wrote the "w" first, then "e," then "n," and finally "i." Then my sense was to pause and let the "d" come after a bit. I looked at the "w-e-n-i" and got nowhere until I simply said it phonetically. "Wen" was the word "when" and "i" was the word "I." I paused. *What did the D mean? What would complete the sentence?* Then I said aloud, "When I . . . ," and I immediately *knew* the answer by the sick feeling I got inside. *When I died. (That was what I know as dissociation.)*

I put down the pen. How young was I "when I died" emotionally? Maybe six months, maybe six years. I don't know. And how many others have "died" in this way, too?

What WENID Means

Withholding: This abuse is WENID at its worse. Withholding means not being given what you need emotionally, mentally, physically, or spiritually to grow. In my case, Mom withheld her unconditional love. I had no emotional support within my family and little attention.

Enabling (Codependency): In my case, it was primarily Dad enabling Mom to do all that she did. He enabled her by coming home late at night, by not being around to see how she was "handling" the children, and by not asking John and me questions about what we'd done that day (or anything else). To some degree, we *all* enabled the pattern by keeping quiet and harboring the things we knew. But Dad *allowed* it, and that was wrong.

Neglect: This abuse is defined by WebMD.com as "...not giving or doing something that a child needs." As the website states: "Emotional abuse is saying or doing things that make a child feel unloved, unwanted, unsafe, or worthless. It can range from yelling and threatening to ignoring the child and not giving love and support. It may not leave scars you can see, but the damage to a child is just as real." The article further stated: "Neglect happens when a child does not get the shelter, schooling, clothing, medical care, or *protection* [emphasis added] he or she needs. Child neglect is just as serious as abuse and is even more common."[5]

---

5. "Health & Parenting: Child Abuse and Neglect," by Healthwise Staff, date last updated November 14, 2014, http://www.webmd.com/parenting/tc/child-maltreatment-topic-overview.

I consider neglect a form of emotional abuse that should be treated as such. Neglect can be hard to see, especially when someone is ignored and little or no yelling is involved. No transfer of energy (good energy) occurs that helps a person develop. *It is the absence or silence that kills.*

In my case, Mom didn't care about me the way a mother should. For example, I sucked my thumb until I was seven years old. (In her defense, she tried to get me to stop.) I also picked my nose until fourth grade when I stopped on my own. Also, in elementary school, I wore the same outfit to school two or three consecutive days a week, and then I'd switch to a second outfit for the remainder of the week. I did this *every week* until the third or fourth grade. It was only then I noticed everybody else showed up wearing something different every day. Wouldn't a mother have been more attentive, more caring? Yet I felt ignored and unprotected—yet it was *her* I needed protection from.

Isolation: In my own definition, I believe isolation means preventing a child from experiencing social interaction—being around other children or adults and seeing how others live. In my case, my school had no kindergarten and no day-care centers were available (that I know of) in my area. We lived about a twenty-minute drive outside of town in a rural neighborhood that had only a few children. I wasn't allowed to play with those children until I was well into elementary school.

Mom had a double standard for John and me. After Mom died, one of the neighborhood kids who knew both of them all those years told me that my brother "could go anywhere and do anything," and that I was not allowed to. He was surprised I didn't know that. But I later realized all of this created an isolation that helped keep the dissociation strong and in place.

In my experience, all four of these abuses—withholding, enabling, neglect, and isolation—overlap. And dissociation—the D in WENID—results.

A Niacin Release Story

Besides the release I experienced through chocolate, I also had a release with niacin (Vitamin B3).

In 2002, I started to notice ads for niacin, a supplement commonly sold at pharmacies, but I'd never purchased it. Yet when something keeps coming to my attention, I know to take action—even today, it happens this way. So I asked my doctor about niacin and other supplements that can be taken without a prescription. She said it was okay to take it but to make sure I didn't take too much of anything because an excess can cause harmful effects.

Next, I went to the drugstore where I stood in the aisle and read the niacin bottles for dosage and side effects, then I chatted with the pharmacist. He said itching tends to be a side effect. Hmmmm. I'd already experienced lots of itching with my chocolate release in 2001.

Then I stood in front of the bottles of niacin for quite a while until I *felt* which one was right for me—one that had a low dosage within the restrictions my doctor had mentioned. I bought it with the absolute intent of taking it when I got home. I paid for it and then walked out of the store. Just as I stepped off the curb to go to my car, there was a big surprise. Although I hadn't taken any of the pills yet, I felt an explosion of little nerve endings along the back of my neck discharge a tingling sensation. I'd never experienced that before. They went off all at once. And just like that, it was over. *Poof!* There were no sounds, but the sensation I felt was enough.

Apparently buying and deciding to take niacin was enough to generate a release from my body. I can't say I felt any different physically after the release, but obviously energy had built up in that area. It didn't need to be stuck there anymore, and a part of me wanted it gone. Taking niacin was going to do the job. Thankfully, I didn't experience any itching at all.

This incident taught me that the way back from dissociation required trusting myself. I had to be willing to follow my intuition to wherever it took me. However, I did set down two limits: I would not break any laws or jump off any bridges.

Another Iceberg Rises Story

While writing this book in 2012, I became aware that another iceberg wanted to come up—yes, another one.

For a few nights, I had felt restless. Then on a Saturday afternoon as I was driving to get groceries and then go exercise, I sensed something wanted to come *now*. So I reached for the only paper I had—my grocery list—in my purse. Before I could write anything, my intuition said, *Go home*. I skipped my plans and headed toward home, but before I got there, words began to surface.

At the next stoplight, I sensed the iceberg rising. Words were written on it. So I narrowed my vision of the iceberg in my mind's eye to read the words and saw, *I was stuck at fifteen/sixteen. I never got out of it until today.* I didn't fully know what that meant, but I knew Dad died when I was sixteen, and at fifteen, I'd had my first thoughts of suicide.

Once I arrived home, I settled into a comfortable chair and focused. More had come up, and I could now "read" the story on the iceberg:

> There was no support at home for anything you wanted to do with your life. There was no support at all. John was being groomed to take over the business and you had better not try to outshine him or get a voice. "I won't allow it," my mother said, and I felt her energetically. She never had to say anything directly; you simply always got the message. I reacted to all of this by choking on all the work I had to do at school. So, I said "no" to forensics, which made my teacher not very happy. I never said why I had to pull back. From then on, that teacher and a few others looked at me differently. They didn't know

what was wrong, but they knew something was. But no one ever asked me. I probably wouldn't have been able to articulate it anyway. You wouldn't have known what words to use when you are being threatened energetically by your own mother. It would have meant taking Mom on and I had no support within the family for that. I was on my own. When Dad died about a year later, I was helplessly on my own now energetically and otherwise. There was no one around to help me. I just "left" the scene. I shrunk back to some fraction of myself, about 40 percent. Other parts had left earlier. Things were not looking good for me at all.

In retrospect, it made sense about the forensics activities. Participating in forensics would have created a line in the sand for Mom because engaging in it would have helped me develop into a stronger, more vocal person, and hence a stronger daughter. As I did in times past when something big like this came up, I went into a period of mourning, quietly secluding myself over the next few days. I knew this revelation required time to sink in so I could make inner adjustments.

I wondered what was at the bottom of the iceberg that might be pushing it up. I looked for any words but found none. However, I sensed something

> *A counselor once said to me, "You are one person." Repeating this statement helped me many times over these years. Yes, I'd had splits, tears, holes, and blockages inside of me—inside my energetic field—that should never have been there. Nor should they exist in anyone.*

was there; I just couldn't read it. So I paused and finally it came. *Directly underneath the iceberg was the age of seventeen.* Pushing. That meant I was growing again and finally leaving fifteen/sixteen behind. A counselor once said to me, "You are one person." Repeating this statement helped me many times over these years. Yes, I'd had splits, tears, holes, and blockages inside of me—inside my energetic field—that should never have been there. Nor should they exist in anyone.

Causes of Dissociation

Situations such as those I've described can cause someone to dissociate. It doesn't take much to dissociate at the physical level, and it takes even less at the soul/energetic level.

The kind of treatment I received can cause people to shut down so they don't die, although they can die *emotionally*. Dissociation is the halfway point to *physically* dying. It can be difficult to return from this point, but people do. And I believe more people would come back if others were there to help them.

When you're not accepted by your own family, it leaves a big hole inside that you are aching to have filled. At first, you're not totally aware of it, but deep inside you know. Unconsciously, you search repeatedly for an answer, but none comes. You go through life emotionally numb, trying to ignore the hole. All of this goes on very early in life when you don't have the cognitive ability to add the words and memories. Still, you *know* something is wrong.

Eventually, you find ways to fit in. "Whatever works" becomes your motto—which puts you in survival mode. *That's how life was for me.* If I could have spoken as an infant, I would have said, "Oh God, why am I even here?"

10

The Unseen World

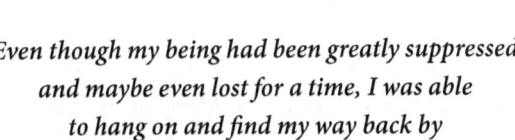

*Even though my being had been greatly suppressed
and maybe even lost for a time, I was able
to hang on and find my way back by
embracing unseen parts of me.*

THIS CHAPTER ADDRESSES INVOLUNTARY PARTS OF yourself that come from an unseen place. Listen; they might be trying to give you a message.

When I was fifteen years old and a sophomore in high school, I experienced thoughts of suicide. But they weren't the "normal" kind. They came from an "involuntary place" within me. A place that is as real as our physical world and can impact our daily life without you realizing it.

Here's what happened.

Suicide Thoughts at Age Fifteen Story

One morning, I was getting ready for school as usual. I stood in the bathroom in front of the sink grooming my eyebrows with a single-edge razor blade (because I didn't know I was supposed to pluck them using tweezers). At some point, I found myself looking down at the blade in my right hand. Suddenly, my eyes seemed to have *a mind of their own*. My gaze moved over to the inside of my left wrist, and I had the thought, *This would be so easy.*

It scared the bejeebers out of me.

Where did that come from? I quickly sat down on the side of the bathtub and paused. *What just happened?* I didn't call out for help. I didn't go to Mom or Dad. I just sat for a bit. Then I decided I wasn't going to school that day.

Next, I opened the bathroom door, walked out onto the balcony over the living room, saw Mom below, and calmly said to her, "I don't feel well, and I'm not going to school today." Then I said, "I think I want to talk with our minister." She looked at me and didn't say anything or ask questions. Finally, she said, "Okay."

My minister was at the Lutheran Church in Lake Geneva. I didn't know him very well, but something inside told me he was the person to reach out to. I called the church that morning and asked if he was available. He would be later in the afternoon, I learned, so I made an appointment.

Psychological counseling had a stigma to it back then, so seeing *that* kind of counselor wasn't an option. Also, in my world, there were few people I could have talked to about this whom Mom would have approved of. In fact, the reverend was the *only* one. So that afternoon, he and I talked for a while, although I had no words to describe my experience to him. All in all, he didn't do much, but talking with him was something.

Although he didn't know me well at all, he knew who I was. His approach was to first ask me to get a transcript from my school so he could see my academic record. It took a few days to get the transcript, but when I showed it to him, he was pleasantly surprised at how well I was doing academically. However, he said I needed to cut back on all my extra-curricular activities. That was about the time my teacher was encouraging me to join forensics—one more extra-curricular activity. So based on the reverend's advice, I backed off the forensics. Ultimately, I noticed that less activity did seem to ease whatever was going on. Part of me apparently wanted "out."

It would be slightly more than a year later when Dad would pass and things in my family got worse.

NSF Program Certificate on My Old Bedroom Wall Story

Dad was buried on a Friday and I left home the following Sunday to attend the National Science Foundation's Summer Science Training Program at the University of Wisconsin–Madison. By then, I was on my way to being a high school senior. I'd been selected as an alternate but a month before Dad died, I was notified that I could attend. The timing to go seemed odd, but no conversation at home took place about my *not* going. The university's large, beautiful campus was where I'd live for approximately six weeks—a world away from Mom and John.

The program proved to be a refuge for me after Dad died. The other students and the staff welcomed me and showed their support. At the end of the program, I received a certificate that I proudly framed. It hung on my bedroom wall in the log cabin for forty-one years.

How did I know that?

In 2006, I went to see John at the log cabin for a fourth time since Mom died—the time I learned that a simple glance is *never* simply a glance.

Mostly, I went there to find memorabilia I'd see for a last time or take with me—if John would allow it. At the time, I felt tension between us because we didn't yet have an agreement regarding Mom's will. We sat in the living room as we had three times earlier in 2005. Then I asked to use the bathroom and John accompanied me up the stairs. Once we reached the top, I looked to the right into Mom's bedroom, then quickly looked to the left toward my old bedroom, now John's. Previously, his door had always been closed. This time, John invited me inside.

The room's wood-paneled walls seemed the same as ever. So did the vaulted ceiling and the wooden beam that stretched across its length. Being a corner room, it had windows on two sides. I noticed the small single closet that never held much.

Then I walked inside the room. It only took a few steps to reach the far edge of my old single bed. For the most part, all the furniture pieces had stayed the same and so had their placement—déjà vu except for the magazines and papers my brother had spread over the floor. They limited the already narrow walkway between the bed and the desk.

Immediately to my left stood my old dresser. For years, my ponytail—cut off in seventh grade—had found a home in one of the drawers. Was it still there? No time to look.

Also to my left, I recognized my old desk—the one I'd used for doing my homework in high school. The bed covers were old and the mattress was still probably mine. Everything looked ratty and worn. Overall, the room was dirty and filled with stagnation. Near the window I noticed John's telescope (he liked astronomy), though it looked like it hadn't been used in a while.

But what caught my attention was the wall above the bed filled only with *my* memorabilia, nothing of John's. Most of it dated back to my high school and college days, including my Augustana College pennant and a few things from high school. Low on the wall near the bed, I noticed the pocketknife marks I'd made in elementary school. The initials and other marks I had carved hadn't been covered in all these years.

I also noticed the certificate I'd been given from the National Science Foundation the summer Dad died. In fact, when I first entered the room, I had *immediately* looked to that wall and glanced at the certificate—the first thing I wanted to see for some reason.

Standing at the other end of the bed, John faced me the entire time. If he caught my initial glance toward the certificate, I didn't notice. But apparently he did. After I excused myself to go to the bathroom and returned, John stood in the same place, but my certificate had disappeared. I instantly looked down to the floor toward the space between the back of the dresser and the wall.

There, I could plainly see the edge of the frame of the certificate almost at my feet. I reached down and grabbed it from behind the dresser. "I'm taking it with me," I said. I'd busted him. He said nothing.

We got specific about other items, including two college mugs and a photo of me as a child sitting on Santa Claus's lap. I took them all. Another photo came from my wedding, and John said he wanted that to stay. All this time, no word was said about why he tried to hide the National Science Foundation certificate. His silence didn't matter to me.

But having the certificate did seem important to a *part* of me, being the first thing I wanted to see. It had significance, and I sensed he knew it. Because I went for it first, apparently I knew it too. My journaling later revealed that it had value because it was from the time when my father died, plus it was related to science journalism, the subject I studied there.

But how did I know John had hidden the certificate and where? And how did I realize it so quickly? *My eyes had a mind of their own* as they followed the vibration of the certificate from the wall to a spot behind the dresser. Yes, my *eyes* found it!

Legs of Cement Story

When I was twelve, every night about nine o'clock I customarily let Panther out for a bathroom break through the basement/garage door. Panther was our black Labrador retriever.

One night before letting him out, I had an ominous feeling that something was about to happen—that I needed to get out of the house. *An obvious warning, it seemed to me.* So after Panther went out, I stepped into the darkness onto the cemented area just outside the door. I waited. Panther did his business and I kept waiting. Nothing happened, although I imagined the house might blow up or something like that. So I waited a bit longer. *Still nothing.* After I took Panther inside, that ominous feeling came over me again. So Panther and I both went out again. *Nothing.*

I actually did this five times. Each time, the same feeling overcame me as I stepped back into the house. Eventually I said "Enough!" and I stayed inside. But while still in the basement, I put my jacket on the coat hook and turned to open the door to go upstairs to the kitchen. Then one step away from the bottom step, my legs froze. Although I could move from the waist up, from the waist down, my legs felt heavy as if stuck in cement. *I couldn't lift them at all!*

Although I knew others were home, I didn't yell for help; I just stood. I waited and wondered. Nothing changed. Finally, I worked with one leg at a time to see if I could get it moving. After a few minutes of trying to lift this dead weight, I was able to place my foot up onto a step. My legs clearly didn't want to go back into the house—though I didn't realize it at the time.

After I finally got one leg to go, I began working with the other. It too gave in and let me place my other foot up onto the step. Gradually, I experienced less and less resistance. I wish I'd more fully understood my deep reluctance to go inside. I remember thinking that I had nowhere else to go—no aunts or

"Involuntary" Events

I call what happened to me in each of these stories "involuntary" events. My eyes moved on their own—and swiftly—as if someone else were looking through them while I was aware of what was happening. My legs froze and wouldn't move, even though my mind commanded them to do so. It seemed as if a whole agenda different from my conscious one was operating. I've since realized that *dissociation* caused that.

Poets say the eyes are the window to the soul. It's true, but that window can also be the legs, the whole body, and what we do and don't do. We may find it difficult to believe that we're more than our physical bodies. However, the experiences I've had—including flashbacks to other lives I've lived—tell me there's clearly more going on than can be seen.

I grew up in the Lutheran Church and then spent time in the Roman Catholic Church. In both, I recited the Nicene Creed, the beginning of which speaks to this point. It states, "We believe in one God, the Father Almighty, Maker of heaven and earth, and of all that is Seen and Unseen..." To me, those words open the door to something more than the physical that isn't seen. It's energy that vibrates at a higher rate than in the physical world.

As Pierre Teilhard de Chardin famously stated, we are spiritual beings having a human experience.

uncles or trusted friends I could turn to. The only family members I had lived in that house—and *they* were the problem.

"Involuntary" Wandering Eyes in the Counselor's Office Story

In 1997, I made my first attempt to seek serious psychological counseling. My divorce had been finalized the year before and counseling was available through my employer, so I signed up for the four free sessions. I even paid for one on my own in 1998.

Beginning again in 2002, I continued seeing the same counselor. During one of our sessions, I found my eyes wandering around her office while she and I talked. At first, I didn't notice my eyes "doing their own thing," even though my head was turned toward her as we talked. It wasn't until she spoke the word *dissociation* that my eyes darted back to her. That's when I realized my eyes had been looking around as if they had a mind of their own. At the time, I didn't connect this experience with what had happened at age fifteen with the razor blade, but the eye movements were the same kind—separate from me, yet still *me*.

Looking back, I believe part of me was checking out her office to see if it was a safe place and also to see what she had on her walls. In many ways, my eyes had wandered exactly like small children sometimes do, looking around until their name is called. Only then do you have their attention and they have yours.

Dissociated parts respond this way, too, or at least mine did. So throughout this period of integration, I used the technique of saying the word *dissociation* to rein them in. I also learned to pay attention to what my eyes were looking at before I said anything to bring them back. Often, I found they were trying to show me or tell me something I needed to know. This happened a lot. *And I learned to make a point of accepting and including all these parts of me.*

It's not easy to stay aware of this throughout the day, but I refuse to allow any parts of me to be separate anymore.

An "Involuntary" Part Speaks Directly to John Story

On my third visit to the log cabin in 2005—the same trip when my missing pieces came home to me—I had another "involuntary" moment involving John that deeply surprised me. It taught me that my "involuntary" part had a voice, too.

Sometime during the visit, I asked to use the bathroom. I climbed the staircase alone to the balcony, glancing into Mom's room to the right and then glancing to the left to see into my old bedroom. John's bedroom door was closed, so I went straight into the bathroom.

After finishing, I walked down the stairs but didn't return to the yellow stuffed chair I'd been sitting in. Instead, I altered my path so I would walk right in front of John, who was sitting in Mom's old recliner. There I stopped.

Turning and looking directly into John's face, I spoke words I'd never even thought of before, but they rolled out of my mouth as if I'd rehearsed them for a lifetime: "I've been one step ahead of you all these years and don't you ever forget it." I said them feeling like Clint Eastwood's Dirty Harry character in the movie *Sudden Impact* when he said, "Go ahead—make my day."

In an instant, I turned again and proceeded toward my chair. John didn't respond, and I said nothing more about it. Our afternoon continued typically as if those words had never been spoken.

11

Relationships That Had to Change

Energetically, I gave my close relationships what I could. I have found that dissociation and close relationships don't go well together.

HAVING BEEN SO CONDITIONED BY THE WASTELAND of emotional support I'd experienced from Mom and John, I would accept little or nothing from my other significant relationships. Therefore, in both my marriage and the "shoehorn" relationship that followed, I stepped into what I was familiar with—distance. Let me set the stage for the stories that follow.

My Twenty-Five-Year Marriage

Mom didn't like my husband. "He has facial hair," she said, referring to his mustache and beard, after I first brought him home. Regardless, trusting my gut, I married him in 1970. The marriage, which lasted twenty-five years, ended in divorce in 1996. Looking back, I realize I married him because I needed a safe place to go.

However, marrying *anyone* when I didn't have a voice made for a non-marriage. I was always simply "making nice" and dancing around what was happening to keep things going, even when I shouldn't have. I eventually realized he wasn't the right man for me. I also realized he wasn't a good husband—or even a good roommate. Still, he offered a "safe harbor" until I could wage the real fight between my mother and me. Unfortunately, that would take a long time—twenty-five years to be exact.

The "Ow" Game Story

We never fought during the entire time of our marriage, but occasionally my husband would grab my arm just above the elbow on the outside. This related to a casual thing or a gentle "come over here" gesture without malice or control. "Ow! That hurt!" I'd immediately say, so he'd stop with a puzzled look on his face. He couldn't understand it and, frankly, never tried. But often it *really* hurt.

After later going through what I did with my chocolate release, I realized this pain was what an emotional energy blockage feels like. Just below this "Ow" point located on the outside of my arm was the inside of my elbow. After my release with chocolate, I had watched my system clean itself out and saw the inside of my elbow turn red, scaly, and itchy—what looked and felt like a toxic waste dump. It reminded me of suffering from eczema in those same locations as a child. My arms looked and felt this way both then and during the chocolate release.

The Last Straw Story

The conversation that ended our marriage lasted only as long as it took to walk three blocks in our neighborhood.

It happened on a regular work day for us as well as a regular school day for our two children. We'd eaten dinner and I was washing the dishes. He was watching television and the children were playing. I remember the early October Wisconsin weather being pleasant that day.

He was aware that issues were coming up between us, and I was pushing them—nothing specific, just clear that something was "going on" with me. As I finished the dishes, he approached me and suggested taking a walk—something new for us. His request surprised me. I agreed.

As we left the house and walked down the driveway, he made

it clear this was a "pre-emptive strike," in his view. I suspect he thought he would nip whatever it was in the bud. At first, we walked without saying a word. Then the conversation started. It was short.

"I want a divorce," I said to him.

"Is there someone else?" he asked.

"Originally there wasn't, but there is now," I replied.

Long silence. Yes, we spoke other words, but they instantly became irrelevant. Before long, we turned around and walked back to the house.

Our divorce itself—considered by outsiders to be amicable compared to many—didn't take long. With Wisconsin being a no-fault divorce state, a four-month waiting period after filing for divorce meets the state's legal requirement. Then I was free. *"Finally!"*

However, experiencing a divorce proved to be only the "warm-up act" for what I would experience with Mom and John.

My husband didn't know that, about three months before, I'd "heard" a door slam in my head. It marked the last straw for me. *I would no longer accept being treated the way he treated me.*

It happened in the late afternoon. We sat fully clothed on the bed in our bedroom after spending the day at an aircraft show in Oshkosh. While there, I had repeatedly attempted to take his hand to hold it, but he kept moving away. Later in our bedroom, I explained that his mother had once shared a precious story with me about his sister and her husband. She'd spoken about his sister's husband's passion for his wife, about how much he loved her hands and how much he loved *her*. Then I asked him, "Why don't you ever tell me you love me?"

He sat there, deadpan. His response sent a shock wave through me. "Because nothing more needs to be said." Then he promptly got up and left the room, went into his bathroom, and shut the door behind him.

SLAM! As he walked by me on his way to the bathroom, I swear I "heard" a door slamming in my head. It was so loud, I thought I'd jump off the bed!

"*He must have heard it, too!*" But he kept right on walking.

That's when a voice inside me said, "*I can't stay.*"

The word "divorce" had never been in my vocabulary, but in the next moment, I clearly "heard" these words: "*If that means a divorce, then so be it—and all that flows from it.*" The involuntary part of me was telling me what to do.

Eventually, he requested counseling, but I refused. I had the strong and absolutely clear gut feeling I must cut this off with a knife. Later, I realized he likely would have tried to drag it out. What I didn't realize was that the "involuntary" part was already at work unraveling the life I'd built since I left the log cabin. The issues with my mother and my dissociation—showdowns far worse than the divorce—would take center stage. In the end, I had to leave not only my husband but my mother and brother as well.

It took me years to realize the last straw wasn't only what my husband had *said* that day in our bedroom. It was also his leaving the room instead of engaging in a conversation with me. By walking away, he declared his refusal to talk about the issues of importance to me.

My path became clear.

My "Shoehorn" Relationship Story

A shoehorn is a small metal or plastic tool that helps slip the heel of a foot into a shoe. In this case, my "shoehorn" helped me "out" of the shoe of my uncomfortable marriage and assisted in my emotional and financial survival. Further, my shoehorn guy, an accomplished attorney, helped me while I stabilized myself and supported me in my fight for what was rightfully mine from my father.

Now retired, he had been one of my instructors in my 1994 IRS training class. In 2005, I hired him to help the lawyers in my estate fight. His experience with the IRS was critical in my situation.

This attorney lived more than eight hundred miles away from me and was also going through a divorce. At one point early on (long before Mom died), we were more than just friends. That lasted a number of months. Eldridge Cleaver once said, "You're either part of the solution or you're part of the problem." He had become part of my solution; my husband had not. However, neither of them recognized my real predicament, which was the shutdown caused by the childhood trauma I'd experienced and the war with my mother and brother. They assumed I was the person they saw on the surface without looking deeper. How could they? I was just learning it myself.

Connecting With Me Story

At the recommendation of my spiritual mentor, I started journaling in 1997. This practice began after I finished law school and divorced but before my chocolate release in 2001.

At first, I thought journaling meant I should keep a diary. *Wrong.* Rather than simply writing about activities of the day, it's meant to delve into my deepest thoughts.

One night, with only paper and pen in front of me, I sat down on the floor in my bedroom, lights on, a candle burning on the nearby nightstand. *What should I write?* Well, whatever came to my mind.

So I wrote about small problems I was facing and brainstormed their solutions on paper. I quickly found this to be a good way to nail a thought so I could let it go and move on to the next thought. Then I let my pen start anywhere it wanted to on the page. I drew things—arrows, circles—anything that symbolized what I was trying to get out. While in the flow, I would have turned the page upside down if that's what I felt my hand wanted me to do.

Eventually, I learned how to ask myself questions. My mentor had taught me to write a question with my dominant hand and then use my non-dominant hand to answer it—no matter how poor my penmanship might be.

Once I got used to journaling, I accidentally (or not!) asked myself a question that has proven to be (for me anyway) the mother of all questions: *What do I need to know?*

I didn't get a lot of answers the first time I asked it. Then sometime later while at my desk in Milwaukee, I *felt* an urge to pull out a new pad of paper and I wrote down my thoughts as they flooded in. They started with the present and began moving into the past. I wrote for the next forty to forty-five minutes with no let up. It *felt* as if someone were telling me things I already knew (sort of) but from a whole new perspective.

That journaling session happened in the morning. In the afternoon around breaktime, the flow of thoughts like a downloading started again and lasted for another forty-five minutes. The stream of information had picked up where it had left off from the morning. In between, I was able to get all my work done.

After I went home and ate dinner, the urge to journal started again—another forty-five minutes' worth. But it didn't end there. *This pattern went on every day for almost three months.* The downloading of information worked its way from present time going backward through my marriage and having children, and then into my childhood. I had thought it would most certainly finish at the point in time when I got married, *but no!* It kept going. These downloads helped me realize how my childhood issues had affected everything I'd done as an adult, right up to the present. *Yikes!* So I kept writing and writing, and I'm glad I did. This source helped me make sense of my past and continues to tell me what I need to know—even today.

So I kept writing and writing, and I'm glad I did. This source helped me make sense of my past and continues to tell me what I need to know—even today.

How to Journal

At first when you journal, you have to be patient with yourself and simply keep writing. Think of it as if you're asking this question of someone you've ignored for years: *What do I need to know?*

You know that person won't readily answer you the first time you ask. So simply keep writing your stream of thought and eventually a *credible* answer will come. How will you know it's credible? Because the answer comes from a different place and makes sense in a way you've likely never thought of before.

At least that's what my journaling eventually became.

12

The Process of Energetic Change

*Early on in this process of change, I felt I'd be living
two lives, and they'd be lived very differently
from each other. So far, that is true.*

My intuition tells me that what I went through in 2001 with my chocolate release should be called the Process of Energetic Change.

Yes, change *is* a process. Given everything that had happened to me and how I responded, it was my path to personal empowerment. No matter how long the dissociation lasted—for decades, in my case—it was the Process of Energetic Change that set me free.

Keys to Changing Energetically

The key to the Process of Energetic Change involves trusting yourself and following the internal directions you get. Allow the process to show you how to clear your internal energetic circuits and get you running the way you always could have—with all of your innate creativity blazing and full self-esteem restored.

Relying on this Process, you begin to grow again, filling in all the blanks. And it doesn't matter how old you are when it starts.

As explained earlier, I experienced an energetic "opening" with my soul coming fully present again. I was "waking up," and the dissociation and blockages began to clear. A new person—*a new whole person*—started to emerge.

In my situation, it took several triggers to start the Process of Energetic Change. I do think timing or readiness is critical, with a specific event or *trigger* outwardly leading the way.

Timing and Triggers

Triggers can be almost any kind of event that causes a lot of stress or trauma: losing a job, making a career change (even a positive one), losing a home or a loved one, dealing with illness, having to relocate, experiencing financial stress, serving in the military and experiencing conflict and war—to name a few. However, the *timing* of the underlying triggering event provides the key.

Two things—my chocolate release and the start of my mother's infirmity—were my big triggers. Both occurred in the same year, 2001. But I recognize I'd been gradually gaining power by trusting myself more and more. At a time when my mother's strength was declining and her physical capabilities diminishing, her power over me began to break up. I started eating chocolate again and, by the end of year, she was bedridden. Not a coincidence. *It was timing.*

However, leading up to my chocolate release, several events signaled that an energetic change was happening. They heralded my energetic awakening from dissociation. That meant I was getting all of "me" back and ultimately gaining my freedom.

I've noted some of these events here in the order they happened.

My family moved back to the Lake Geneva area in 1984. My husband accepted a position about an hour away from Lake Geneva (Rockford, Illinois). When housing became a problem for us in 1984, my mother offered us one of her rental properties, saying we could rent it for a year. I didn't want to go there, but deep inside I *felt* it was the right thing to do. We took the offer, ended up staying four years, and then moved on. Lake Geneva was a place I swore I'd never go back to, but moving back proved to be the right thing to do because I got to see that things hadn't changed in all those years.

I was accepted to Marquette University Law School in 1988. I followed my inner direction in late 1986, and one of my out-of-the-blue thoughts told me *I needed to go to law school in order to become the person I always could have been.*

I divorced my husband of twenty-five years in 1996. I trusted my gut feelings that I had to leave. I'd found the courage to do so without knowing all of the reasons behind why my leaving felt necessary.

I learned to journal and meditate in 1997. These practices immeasurably helped me understand my inner self and eventually led me to my Deep Self. I've been journaling and meditating ever since.

I sought the assistance of a professional counselor in 1997. The amazing information I received in my sessions started me on a quest to learn more about myself. My counselor validated many of the things I was wondering, but I had no answers for the questions she asked of me. Getting counseling provided an important step in the right direction.

The chain bracelets I wore began to fall off. I often wore gold chain bracelets—simple ones, not the fancy kind, and I'd usually wear only one at a time. In the years leading up to the 2001 chocolate release, the bracelets began to fall off for no apparent reason. I never found two of them because I never felt them fall off. Another one was a S-link bracelet with a sturdy clasp. I saw this one fall off—right into the toilet. It took me a while to understand this as a sign of my energy dynamic changing. It could be said *I was breaking my chains.*

I quit my cubicle job at the IRS in 2000. From 1994 to 2000, I was an estate and gift tax attorney for the IRS in Milwaukee. Although it was a good job, I had to work in a cubicle, which seemed stifling. After my divorce in 1996, the job was my sole support *and* I was paying child support for my one child still under age eighteen. I could have had this job longer, but as I changed, I became more and more restless. In my earlier jobs, I'd never stayed long because I'd generally learn everything I need (looking back) and then want more. Going to law school and becoming a tax attorney helped the boredom issue because, finding the subject matter so vast, I knew I'd always be challenged. However, the *something wasn't right* stirrings weren't going away.

So in early 2000, I asked to work part time to pursue writing as a career. My request was granted. Then came my fifty-second birthday in mid-August. I drove to the Milwaukee airport and parked at the north end of the runway at an observation area. I often did personal paperwork there while sitting in my car. Usually a fair number of other people were sitting in their cars like me, hanging out to watch the planes land and take off. Why did I love it? It gave me something to do and a place to go. It also represented *arriving* and *leaving*.

After I'd done some of my personal work, I remember noticing my eyes drift over to the calendar I had open. That's when I heard in my head these words: *So when do you want to quit?* I protested. *Oh God. I can't quit.* Then silence until I heard: *If you were to quit, when would you do it? How much time do you need to give them?* That prompting told me where I was headed. I looked at the calendar, knowing two weeks' notice was customary. *Okay, early September and I'd be done.*

The next day, a Monday, I walked in to my supervisor's office and handed him my resignation. As I recall, he wasn't surprised. We'd gotten along well, and he was always happy with my work, but I think he sensed a change coming. Plus he was a fan of

Thoreau, which I think fit right in to what he saw going on with me as I developed my freedom and self-reliance.

Within two weeks, I left without another job lined up, knowing I'd rely only on my savings for financial support.

I experienced patterns of healing. During the months after quitting my job, the more I journaled and meditated, the more I began to experience patterns of healing. One I call "the slingshot" because it made me feel as if I was backsliding instead of going forward. I'd go back to old ways and habits until I couldn't stand it anymore (like pulling the sling of the slingshot back, back, and back until it's strained). Then a part of me would shoot forward with a whole lot of new emotional growth (letting go of the sling and allowing the projectile to fly through the air to its target).

Here's another pattern I experienced. Starting around 1998, as a Friday night would approach, I'd feel myself become sad and depressed. I had no social life at that time, and I'd just wallow in that fact. On the weekend, I'd rest, cry, and go with the depression instead of fighting it. But because I worked full time Monday through Friday, sometime Sunday afternoon I could feel I was "done," and the real me began to surface. By Sunday night, I felt better and was refreshed enough to do the week of work.

After a series of these weekends, I noticed I was changing. I felt better. I would speak of things from a higher point of view (the high road) instead of negatively (the low road). Later on, all it would take was maybe a day (or two) or a few hours and I'd see a change in the words I use to describe what happened—increasingly more "high road" in tone.

I learned early on *not* to try stopping the backsliding, knowing that it would eventually propel me forward to a better place. Once I'd learned that, this pattern worked every time, and I was glad I'd gone with it. *Knowing and doing this has become a powerful tool.*

I recognize that patterns like this still come up every so often when I experience new growth.

I experienced emotional dams blowing up. Because of having more time for myself, memories would pop into my head for no apparent reason—things I hadn't thought about for years.

At first, some felt nasty, but if I waited, good memories often followed. That meant I'd just blown up an energy blockage—a dam. And like an actual dam being blown up, first the crappy black stuff flows, and then everything trapped behind it gets freed up to flow. Sometimes I didn't notice the crappy stuff except for feeling "off," or I'd become pissed off for no apparent reason. Then, when the good memories started popping, I knew I'd blown a blockage, a dam, for sure.

I found the dam-breaking process brought me to a new emotional place in which I could articulate my past much better. It let me talk about it with new emotional distance, and my view of it had changed for the better.

Dams can also be a lot like frozen puddles. When a dam begins to go, it tends to go all at once, but what *precedes* it is often the critical event. Here's a childhood experience that helped me understand this process.

Typically, spring comes late in the year to Wisconsin. During March, we still have many puddles that are frozen. But as the ground gradually thaws under them, the ice there (the dam/blockage) also begins to thaw and seep into the ground. I loved to "test" frozen puddles on my way to the bus stop or in the schoolyard at recess. Every day I could, I'd walk on one looking for a sign it would crack. Nothing would happen day after day. Then the day came when by applying the slightest amount of pressure with my foot, the surface of the frozen puddle would give way and sink in. Nothing was left underneath it for support; the dam/blockage was gone. *The moment I waited for!*

As a kid, I loved the feel of it giving way accompanied by a kind of deadened crunching sound. That's an example of the dam-breaking process in slow motion.

Dealing with my Wisconsin past has led to many dams/blockages giving way—some with lots of fanfare and others more quietly. But always the same. It gave way to feeling relief on the other side of the release. This pattern of growth continues to this day.

I painted my toenails! In late 2000 while sitting at home, I looked down at my toes. My nails weren't manicured or polished. *I'm going to start wearing nail polish on my toes.* Because I now get pedicures regularly, I'd feel naked today without my toes painted. Back then, this was quite a shift as I generally never wore toe nail polish. It was something other people did, not me.

I made alignment changes, including where I live. I reviewed my friends as well as my jobs, banks, investments, and charge cards to see if they aligned with the new emerging me. Some yes, some no. Thus many of these got to stay; some had to go. Attending law school, divorcing, and leaving my IRS position were all part of making the changes necessary to align with my true, Deep Self.

Further, it became increasingly clear where I was living wasn't right for me. I needed more light and wanted warmth. Wisconsin just didn't cut it! Being in the proper latitude and longitude was important to me, yet I had it wrong for years.

Restoring Alignment

Understanding alignment is a lot like understanding your car and the tires you have on it. All of them should be in perfect alignment with each other so you can steer the car straight down the road and not veer to the left or right. If you hit the curb a few times while parking, you can knock the tires out of alignment, and once they're out, you need to have them realigned.

Energetically, people are like this, too. If you take a few knocks, you can be forced or pushed out of alignment. And if it isn't corrected quickly, you can go down the road of life this way—badly out of alignment!

However, it can take a lot to get back into proper alignment—especially if the knocks went on for years as mine did. But with an open mind and a lot of time and courage, it can be done. The Rules of Energy Flow (introduced in Chapter Three) helped me a lot, as did the journaling and meditation.

Energetically, living in Hawaii and then California has worked much better for me than being in Wisconsin.

I severed all connection with my brother John. He was told not to contact me. If he should ever need to, he was instructed to do so through the lawyers.

13

My View of All of "This"

*I didn't know I could react to emotional abuse like
I did, and I didn't know my energetic response (my
reaction) could affect me the rest of my life.*

"THIS" REFERS TO EXPERIENCING ABUSE EARLY ON IN life and then (lucky for me) naturally coming out of my reaction years later. I never knew I'd experienced abuse until I read a pamphlet in 1997—at age forty-nine—while sitting in a counselor's office. It described what I had experienced. It gave it a name. The title on the pamphlet was "Emotional Abuse."

The more I read, the more I was shocked. That realization was a game-changer.

It is my belief that, as hard as people may try to empower themselves, some may have issues similar to mine and therefore may find the task of empowering themselves difficult, if not impossible. *Abuse & Energy* exposes what I experienced both as a child and as an adult and how I responded (reacted). My reaction included dissociation (psychological numbing and disengagement), energy blockages (mostly emotional), an allergy to chocolate caused by emotional distress, and a loss of pieces of my energetic self (my soul) at an early age. This book details how this reaction began to end at the age of fifty-two. That point marked the start of the kind of growth that should have occurred in my twenties and thirties. It hadn't. I had missed it. I'm convinced that knowing this information can help people.

What was the key to this empowering growth? Finding ways to *end my reaction* to all I'd experienced.

What Does It Mean to "Be" Energy?

The most important factor is knowing that energy *does not die;* therefore, *we* don't die either. Yes, our bodies give out, but our souls do not. Perhaps that is what is meant by the term "eternal life." They have a different kind of life span.

Souls themselves do not have a gender, nor do they have a specific color. Souls can express themselves in a multitude of ways. No color, no race, no gender, no specific religion or faith, and no specific sexual preference can be used to describe a soul. A soul is a soul; it's energy—a being of light—that expresses itself

> **Underneath it all, we are all the same.**

according to the circumstances it finds itself in while in physical form. Therefore, underneath it all, we are all the same.

Opens a Door for Discussion

Honestly, I am happy to have the events of this story behind me. Trusting my gut has gotten me here safely, and it will carry me forward as I continue to grow.

This book opens a door for a discussion of energy. Abuse is my starting point for this discussion. Why? Because that's where my own story began. Abuse harms souls mercilessly, and it does it far more easily than we think. Dissociation was a major part of my reaction to emotional abuse. It is my belief we all have emotionally shut down in various degrees, some more than others. Hence, it's highly likely we've all experienced dissociation to some degree. The question then becomes, "Has it been rectified *or is it still there?*"

Let me ask you these questions:

- Can you *feel* the way you see others feel or hear others talk about feeling?
- Do you sense that something is wrong, but you never knew quite what it was?
- Do your eyes sometimes wander on their own as if they had a life of their own?

- If the answer is yes to any of these, this suggests you've experienced an energetic reaction at some time in your life. Consider looking into it further. If it is still operating, that means it may be difficult to become fully empowered and therefore have a complete life. *Your reaction may be different than mine, but examining my story opens a door for discussing it.*

**Energy was my Problem and
Energy was the Solution.**

Use My Story as a Case Study

In my view, there needs to be a change in how we think of ourselves—that is, we need to understand *we are energy*. This allows for a shift in both our overall view and treatment of others, and in how we view and treat ourselves. This shift also would enhance how we do the day-to-day tasks of putting food on the table, a roof over our heads, and clothing on our backs.

Trusting yourself and your intuition enhances all of life. So does:

- Knowing the Rules of Energy Flow,
- Understanding how energy blockages (that can later turn into physical blocks within your body) can start in childhood,

- Realizing reactions to experiences you had early in life (or even later) can be hurting you now,
- Recognizing that your energy can drastically shift when the circumstances you once reacted to begin to change, and
- Comprehending that, with all of its triggers and subtleties, there is a Process of Energetic Change. Knowing that can help keep you calm when everything else seems to be changing and *you don't understand why.*
- These truths have come out of *my* story to smooth the way for *your* empowerment. Empowerment begins when the reaction ends.

*Empowerment begins
when the reaction ends.*

14

Empowering Ways That End Reactions

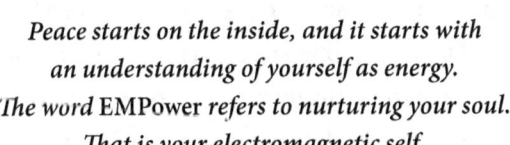

*Peace starts on the inside, and it starts with
an understanding of yourself as energy.
The word EMPower refers to nurturing your soul.
That is your electromagnetic self.*

NURTURING YOUR SOUL TAKES TIME AND EFFORT—
but it is worth it! Nurturing at this very deep level ends reactions and then empowers You and Your light.

I've listed activities below that will serve you by empowering you. They can give you the start you need to restore yourself to your fullest self. They will help you "right" your ship.

Nurturing self-care is the key. This list helped pave the way for me to come back from *my* reaction. I especially recommend the first thirty-one that are listed. But if you can only do one thing, choose this one: TRUST YOUR GUT.

- Trust your gut and your intuition and learn how to set intentions for yourself. I do this. (It can take some practice, but don't be afraid. It's easier than you think.)
- Learn to meditate and journal. (It's critically important. Journals need not be expensive. Look around in your local stores. Often I just use a pad of paper.)
- Own your reaction. Once you own it, you can dismantle it and end it.
- Seek a skilled counselor, preferably one trained in EMDR (Eye Movement Desensitization and Reprocessing). Most important, look for the person your gut says is right for you. (Counseling is covered by many health insurance plans today and EMDR works.)
- As you begin to open up, don't be afraid of the changes that seem to naturally come. Lots of them will seem strange, even odd. (That is just how it is.)
- Do picture puzzles. (Puzzles with five hundred or one thousand pieces worked well for me and still do.)
- Stare at the ceiling, a wall, or just out the window, as needed. It may look like you aren't doing anything, but I can tell you, you are and it will help.
- Have private time, as much as you can get at first and then as needed.
- Have quiet time, as much as you can have at first. You may always need it. It gives balance.

- Once you begin to connect deep inside by meditating and journaling, expect to experience pinging like I did. (The *9/11 Tragedy Story* and the *USS Greeneville/The Crystal Coffin Story* attest to that.) You'll want to keep paper and pen/pencil within reach. Commonly, I have them in every room of the house.
- Learn more about enabling and withholding.
- Learn more about what isolation can do to you.
- Learn more about neglect and what it does to you.
- Learn more about allergic reactions—check with your doctor to find out if yours might be emotionally triggered like mine was.
- Retrieve any lost pieces—refer to the *Missing Energy Pieces Story* in Chapter Two for how I found mine.
- Self-educate on anything you want. It serves to empower you. (Education is the silver bullet for many people.)
- Find role models who are positive, not controlling. (I inadvertently used my mother as a partial role model. I thought I hadn't, but I did. I have changed it.)
- Exercise. (Exercise means getting energy out that has built up inside.) Exercise with others; participate in a yoga, Pilates, and/or Tai Chi class. Alternatively, get videos and do your favorites at home. Dancing is good, too.
- Make lots of friends who are willing to listen.
- Add color to your life.
- Add movement to your life.
- Add texture to your life.

- Add music to your life. Each of these four—color, movement, texture, and music—are foundational to life for energy beings (souls) like us. All of these are important to you, but one of these is the most important. (For me, that one is color. Post-its and washcloths gave me the color I needed at the office and at home at a price I could afford when I didn't have much to spend.)
- Keep your home clean and organized. It helps your peace of mind and can be important for your health.
- Be willing to accept and experience help wherever it comes from. Other people, books, angels, and spirits are recognized good sources. Be prepared to be challenged with unwanted attention from other spirits. You can learn how to handle this easily.
- Study the human energy system using books and charts that display the chakras, meridians, and energy pressure points.
- Learn about nutrition and eat foods that best support your body, health, and energy. Note your body's reactions to specific foods. Your intuition can guide you to foods that best support your personal recovery based on your individual needs.
- Take probiotics every day to clean out any gastrointestinal imbalance inside and promote a healthy interior.
- Limit caffeine and sugar so you know how your body feels without these substances.
- Take digestive enzymes to assist the stomach. (They may not be needed every day.)

- Beautify your environment with cut flowers and plants. Every time you see one, it will remind you to stay open—to not close up.
- Burn candles or incense with smells that you enjoy.
- Relax and enjoy sitting by a fireplace in your home or elsewhere.
- Hang soothing, uplifting, and colorful artwork you like on your walls. Even inexpensive artwork serves this purpose. Consider creating your own.
- Use pens or pencils that flow and make sure everything you use is in good working condition.
- Put yourself in as much natural light as you can whenever you can to receive Vitamin D from the sunlight. Sunlight cleanses and purifies. It will lift your spirits no matter how negative they may have become.
- Smile and laugh whenever you can. This will lift your spirits.
- Hydrate from both the outside and the inside. Moisturize your face and body. Use Vaseline as needed on nail cuticles, hands, and lips—or Chapstick on the lips—to seal moisture into your skin. Use a humidifier if the air is dry. Hydrating from the inside especially requires drinking plenty of water all day long. Energy can't flow when the riverbed is dry!
- Drink teas, especially green and herbal, and have drinks with a bit of carbonation every now and then. Green tea in particular is a natural detoxifier, but both kinds serve to relax you as they assist in energy flow. However, limit sodas (both sugared and sugar-free) to only an occasional indulgence.

- Get into nature and go walking, running, or hiking. Swim outdoors, if possible, or indoors if you can't. Being in nature will provide balance and nurturing.
- Have regular checkups with your primary care physician, eye specialist, dermatologist, and dentist.
- Get massages regularly (every two weeks, if you can, especially if you accumulate stress in your body easily). Do stretches or self-massage at home between professional massages. Locate massage schools that can provide quality massages at an affordable rate.
- Go to a chiropractor for adjustments as needed. Be sure the chairs in your home—and especially the one at your desk—provide proper body support.
- Get a facial (once a month, if you can) if for no other reason than to relieve the stress in your face. Alternatively, give yourself face massages regularly.
- Have pedicures and manicures for better energy flow out your hands and feet.
- Take a bath using Epsom salts once a week to restore and maintain your levels of magnesium. It will cleanse your aura, calm your nerves, and rejuvenate your skin.
- Get a Reiki healing on your body from a Reiki energy-healing practitioner.

This list is simply a start. You'll find more at my website at www.MarianeWeigley.com. Click on Resources. The possibilities are endless. Your goal? To empower yourself so your reaction ends.

Conclusion
Peace Begins On The Inside And Nowhere Else

*Trusting yourself to know what you need to know (and want to know) so you can empower yourself is one of the most difficult things you'll ever do. Remember, the word **EMPower** refers to your ElectroMagnetic Power. Nurture Yourself!*

At times, a change in the daily events of your life can signal a shift is occurring at a deeper level. It's important to pay attention to these sometimes subtle and sometimes not-so-subtle events, as the following stories indicate.

The Pencil Story

Sometime before 2001, I had trouble hanging on to a pencil. I know that sounds ridiculous, but honestly, I'd put one in my hand

and keep dropping it. This "involuntary" dropping lasted between twenty-four and forty-eight hours, which happened to be right before a scheduled appointment with my spiritual mentor. Once I arrived at the appointment and she started talking, in my mind's eye I was suddenly in either Ireland or England a long time ago, in a past life. I was standing in a one-room structure that was poorly built. I could see daylight coming through the wooden slats.

The room was filled with fifteen to twenty children. I was teaching both boys and girls (but mostly girls) the basics of reading and writing. This wasn't allowed at the time, so we had to hide deep in a green forest. It must have been summer or spring as I saw no snow. As I was teaching, I had a pointer in my hand—the "pencil" I kept dropping before this facilitated vision came to me.

Then I could hear horses coming at a full gallop. The men on the horses didn't want the children, especially the girls, to learn anything and had been ordered to put a stop to this. As far as they were concerned, this would be my last day of teaching at this school—or any school, for that matter.

I sensed what was coming. I shooed the children out the door and into the woods, and then I stayed behind to greet the horses with their riders.

The next thing I saw was blood on the wood floor. I could see my left hand feebly trying to write letters in my own blood. And that was the end of the vision.

After that, I understood why I kept dropping the pencil. I've learned that when a past life is coming forth to be revealed and healed, odd things can get one's attention. And there's usually something that needs to be known. For me, it meant I was a teacher then and am becoming a teacher again.

After that, my pencil-dropping stopped. "Your Inside World creates Your Outside Reality." Message received and understood.

> *Your Inside World creates Your Outside Reality.*

Two Places at Once Story

Before 2001 but earlier than the "pencil" episode, I experienced a different kind of flashback not involving my spiritual mentor. I was alone at night in my first apartment in Waukesha, and a thunderstorm was raging outside. While I was walking from my living room to my bedroom through a short hallway, a large bolt of lightning flashed, followed by a terrific thunderclap. I turned to the right to look down a side hallway toward the window in a second bedroom.

In that moment—at the sound of the thunderclap—I was in two places at the same time. I knew I was in my apartment and what year it was, but I was also in a dark dungeon-like place—probably a castle—somewhere in Europe, I felt. Torches hung on either side of my hallway and the short hallway. While looking toward the second bedroom and its window, I was also standing in a hallway in the castle looking toward a room that was something like a library. Then, too, it was nighttime and a loud thunderstorm raged. As I walked closer to my bedroom, I could still sense the torches that lit my way. It felt real because it was.

What do flashbacks generally mean? An awakening can start with odd experiences as we're growing energetically and are "restoring" to our full selves. Giving ourselves permission to experience these kinds of events and not fear them is one of the best things we can do to care for ourselves.

Golden Globe Vision Story

At about three in the morning on October 20, 1999, I was asleep in my bed at my first apartment in Waukesha when something awakened me. I felt a touch on my right wrist by what seemed to be someone's fingers, but no one was there. Without opening my eyes or even moving, I immediately "saw" a yellow/white area straight ahead of me. It looked like a round circle, a golden globe, and I saw it open like a camera lens. I recognized seeing something similar to the yellow/white area in meditation, but it had never opened before.

A vision was starting to form in the globe.

With my eyes still closed, I could clearly see a person standing before me. Presumably, the person was female because I could see that her arm was slender. She was wearing a garment with long brown sleeves. Her skin was white, and her right hand was pointing downward as if she were speaking to someone. She was standing in a room in front of a white wall.

The globe shifted slightly to the right and the aperture widened so I could see even more. The woman's arm then moved upward toward her face, which was out of view. I could see her move, but I couldn't see her face, and I never did.

I sensed this action was actually happening now, but I didn't know if it occurred in the past, present, or future. I couldn't identify the woman for certain. However, it *felt* like the future, and *I was the woman.*

Remember this about energy:

- This physical world (the world you do see) can teach you everything you need (or want) to know about energy (the unseen world).
- Your pain—your "wail"—resides inside your subconscious, your "whale."
- We name things what we do for a reason that is grounded in fundamental energy (the unseen world).
- I'm dedicated to helping you see inside your "whale" and "right your ship" as I continue to "right" my own. Through my writings, I offer Information, Validation, and Support that provide nurturing so your soul can breathe freely in this physical form within the safety it seeks.
- Allow my stories to shed light and possibly provide answers to questions you may have. Look for more

instructive stories in Book Two, *The Involuntary*. It reveals how the ever-adjusting soul releases while in physical form.

- You are more than you *think* you are. You know more than you *think* you do.
- Trust your gut!

You are more than you think you are.
You know more than you think you do.
Trust your gut!

About the Author

Jacob Hand Photography

AS AN INTUITIVE WHO SENSES ENERGY IN A VARIETY of ways, Mariane E. Weigley writes, speaks, teaches, and publishes what it means to be an energy being, a being of light. She writes her story from the soul's perspective—that is, everything is about energy.

She received her BBA in business and education from the University of Wisconsin–Madison in 1973 and earned her JD from Marquette University Law School in 1992. Following her divorce from a twenty-five-year marriage and realizing she "didn't have a life," she turned to counseling, meditation, and journaling. This work resulted in a profound shift at the age of fifty-two. As part of her healing process, she began to write—to heal herself and ultimately lay the groundwork for helping others. The result is *Abuse & Energy*, the first in her series on energy and abuse. Weigley Publications is becoming a hub for information about energy beginning with this focus on abuse.

Mariane was born in southeastern Wisconsin where she lived most of her life. She resides in Northern California.

www.MarianeWeigley.com

www.ingramcontent.com/pod-product-compliance
Lightning Source LLC
Chambersburg PA
CBHW052019290426
44112CB00014B/2305